PENGUIN BOOKS

TRIAL BY FIRE

Neelam and Shekhar Krishnamoorthy are the parents of Unnati and Ujjwal, who lost their lives in the Uphaar Cinema fire.

PRAISE FOR THE BOOK

'The Krishnamoorthys are a shining beacon in the darkness around us. The story of their struggles is an inspiration for all—to overcome adversity with courage, to always fight the good fight'—Rajdeep Sardesai

T0158273

TRIAL BY FIRE

THE GUT-WRENCHING STORY OF THE PARENTS
WHO LOST THEIR CHILDREN TO THE UPHAAR
CINEMA FIRE AND LIVED TO FIGHT FOR JUSTICE

NEELAM AND SHEKHAR
KRISHNAMOORTHY

PENGUIN BOOKS

An imprint of Penguin Random House

PENGUIN BOOKS

USA | Canada | UK | Ireland | Australia
New Zealand | India | South Africa | China

Penguin Books is part of the Penguin Random House group of companies whose
addresses can be found at global.penguinrandomhouse.com

Published by Penguin Random House India Pvt. Ltd.
4th Floor, Capital Tower 1, MG Road,
Gurugram 122 002, Haryana, India

First published in Penguin Books by Penguin Random House India 2016

10 9 8 7 6 5 4 3 2

ISBN 9780143425830

Typeset in Sabon by Manipal Digital Systems, Manipal
Printed at Replika Press Pvt. Ltd, India

www.penguinbooksindia.com

For Unnati and Ujjwal,
with whom we spent the loveliest seventeen and
thirteen years of our lives,
and in whose memory we have spent the most traumatic
nineteen years of our lives, seeking justice.

Prologue

On 13 June 1997, I booked tickets for the matinee show for *Border* for my two lovely teenaged children, Unnati and Ujjwal. In a sense, these were the tickets to their deaths in the terrible man-made fire that engulfed Uphaar Cinema, located in posh south Delhi.

That June morning in 1997, I did what any loving mother would do for her children. It started off as just another day in our lives. We were a family of four, Shekhar and I, successful in our professional lives, blessed with two wonderful children. We were a close-knit family that was happy by all measures of conventional assessment. We couldn't have asked for more then.

It was that time of the year when we usually planned a family vacation. However, since Unnati, our elder daughter, was applying to colleges and was enrolled for a course in the Institute of Company Secretaries, apart from preparing for the SAT, we had decided to postpone our holiday. Ujjwal had been promoted to class nine and was enthusiastically waiting to join senior school. He spent his summer attending swimming and music classes. He also had planned to watch many movies with his friends. We wanted to hire a tutor to coach him in Hindi, but Unnati asked us to wait for the vacation to finish before her little brother was subjected to academics again. We agreed with her and decided to hire a tutor after his school reopened.

Shekhar and I would go to the gym together every day. On 13 June I did not go with him because I had to go to the hospital as my brother-in-law had undergone a bypass surgery. Before leaving, I went to the children's room to say bye to them, but they were fast asleep. They slept like angels and I did not wish to disturb them, so I just kissed them and left. At around 9.30 a.m., Unnati called me up, demanding to know why I had not said bye to them before leaving. I explained that since I left very early, I did not want to disturb them. She wasn't convinced and I found myself apologizing to her. She then reminded me to book tickets for them for the matinee show of the newly released movie *Border*. I assured her that I would personally call the manager of Uphaar Cinema after 10 a.m., once the booking counter opened.

Just like I promised her, I called up the manager and arranged for two tickets for the matinee show. Shekhar picked me up from the hospital in the afternoon and the four of us had lunch together that day. None of us knew then that it was the last meal we would have together as a family. After lunch, Unnati planted a loving kiss on my cheek; I forgot to wipe off the mark her lipstick left on my skin. Unnati noticed this just before leaving the house and commented, 'Mom you still have my lipstick on.'

I had no clue that this was the last time Unnati would ever kiss me.

We left for our office after lunch only to hear some really good news—one of the importers from Europe was appointing us as their agent in India. At around 5.30 p.m.,

I spoke to one of my friends who was a company secretary in a multinational firm, requesting her to help and advise Unnati since she was wondering if she should become a company secretary. She asked me to send Unnati to her office for practical training from Monday—16 June 1997. Shekhar and I left the office to meet a friend of ours, a fashion designer, to discuss Unnati's wardrobe makeover as she would join college soon. Then we went to check on my brother-in-law in hospital again.

At around 7.30 p.m. I called the landline at home hoping to speak to the kids, but there was no response. I paged Unnati to find out their plans and whereabouts. When she did not respond, we panicked and I called up Uphaar Cinema, ignorant of what had happened there.

Unnati's friend, Vishal, contacted us and we learnt that there had been a massive fire at Uphaar. The minute we heard the news, we rushed to the hospital—only to discover that our life had come to a dreadful standstill. Both our children were dead and they had taken with them the perfect life we had worked so hard for, which we had cherished so dearly.

This nightmarish turn of events destroyed us completely and changed our lives forever.

Nineteen years later, the intense feelings of loneliness, sadness, loss, dejection and the wish to die still remain as strong as they were the day everything happened. Nothing has changed and time has not healed our wounds. All our dreams died with our children. We have learnt first-hand the tragic truth that the demise of one's children can never be equated with any other loss; the pain never ceases. We can never erase the memories of our children. Every child leaves an indelible stamp on the lives of their parents; even if they pass away, the parents continue to live with memories and the grief of loss, substituting their physical presence with the all too painful, but constant reminder of their absence. In a sense, time has stood still for us in the last nineteen years and the pain will only leave us when we finally breathe our last.

From 13 June 1997, our lives have just been a tragic journey of indescribable loss, grief and mourning. We have tried to rebuild our broken lives by seeking justice from a system that has let us down again and again. The battle for justice stretches on interminably as we write this, we know not for how much longer.

It took only a few minutes for our children to die, but it has taken us more than nineteen years to get any form of justice for them. In these nineteen long years India has elected four governments, had seventeen chief justices and four prime ministers.

We must confess that although our purpose in writing this book was to share our experiences with readers, this is by no means a tell-all book. Neither have we tried to sensationalize our grief, loss, trauma or challenges nor have we been able to expose everything that we wanted to. Too many facts are still concealed because this book may never have seen the light of day had we exposed them. Often we wondered whether we should name and shame the people who had let us down in the fight for justice. Much against our will, we had to compromise and leave some individuals unnamed, and several facts camouflaged and untold, in the interest of being able to tell a larger part of our story. While we wait for justice in this lifetime, perhaps the entire story will be told only after we are no longer alive.

1

Shekhar and I, Starting a Family

Shekhar (whose official name is R. Krishnamoorthy) and I met in 1977. My sister Manju was hosting a party, to which Shekhar had been invited by a mutual friend. At some point in the merrymaking, Shekhar was asked to sing as his friends knew that he was gifted with a fine voice and could render Bollywood hits from yesteryear with great aplomb. I was struck by his beautiful timbre and we soon found ourselves meeting frequently. I had just turned eighteen and Shekhar was only a year older than me. Our careers were still in their nascent stages. We wanted to marry within a year, in 1978, but Shekhar's family was strongly opposed to the idea of him tying the knot with a north Indian. Hence, we quietly registered our marriage in Delhi.

A year later, we discovered that I was expecting our first child. We both wanted a daughter. Deep down in my heart I was certain the child would be a girl. I was so convinced of it that I even thought of a name for the little girl, before she was born—'Unnati', which means progress. I prepared for her arrival with great excitement and everything I bought for her was pink.

I was admitted to AIIMS because my gynaecologist had advised me to undergo a caesarean; Unnati was a breech child. The operation was scheduled for 31 August. The night before, when Shekhar came to visit me, we decided to watch a late-night film at Uphaar Cinema, as it was the closest theatre to the hospital. This was to be our final escapade before we were sucked into the world of bringing up a child. However, with the surgery a mere forty-eight hours away, neither the hospital nor my mother would have permitted me to go out for a movie. Therefore, we had to trick everyone around us; we told them that we were going home for short while and would be back soon.

As soon as we were out of the hospital, we headed to Uphaar to catch a late show of *Kala Patthar*. After the movie, Shekhar dropped me at the hospital, but I stayed up reading a book. I suddenly started experiencing labour pains. Fortunately for me, a caesarean was not required and I had a normal delivery. There was no way for us to have known that Uphaar, which we had considered safe enough to visit only a few hours before our daughter's birth, would be the very spot where our children would be brutally and cruelly snatched away from us.

When I finally delivered little Unnati, my gynaecologist was surprised that the only question I asked was what was the colour of the baby's eyes. I had always hoped my children would have light eyes like me. She was surprised that I did not ask her about the baby's gender; she did tell me that the baby girl did not have light eyes.

Our lives were filled with great joy after Unnati's birth and she brought a lot of happiness to our home. We were doting parents and called her 'Niti baba', a short and adoring abbreviation of her name. She was an adorable and loving child—always smiling and cheerful, a fast learner and very inquisitive. Extremely friendly, she would reveal everything about the family to any guest who happened to visit us, a habit that earned her the nickname 'BBC' for her broadcasting skills.

Since my mother-in-law was a strict vegetarian, she was averse to non-vegetarian food being cooked in the house. If we wanted non-vegetarian food, we would cook it in her absence. Unnati was very fond of certain kinds of meat. But the child, unaware of the complications that would ensue, would always inform her grandmother that Mama had cooked mutton and chicken for her, often getting Shekhar and me into trouble.

She was also very eager to go to school and actually followed her school-going cousin one day—she went and sat in the car that used to drop her cousin to school. Realizing how keen she was to learn, I got her admitted into a kindergarten school. Thus, at the young age of three, she was admitted to Delhi Public School, East of Kailash. She enjoyed school so much that she never bothered us with the usual excuses and tantrums that so many children use to try and get out of attending school.

We had our share of scary moments too. One day, the autorickshaw that used to pick her up from the bus stand and bring her home after school, met with an accident. She was rushed to AIIMS along with the other children who were travelling in the vehicle. Shekhar and I knew nothing of this and we were extremely anxious when she did not come home on time. We rushed to the bus stand to check if all was well. Some bystanders there told us that a vehicle carrying schoolchildren had met with an accident and all of them had been taken to AIIMS. When we reached the hospital, the doctor treating the children complimented Unnati and told us she was a very brave girl. She was the only child who had not cried in the hospital. The moment she saw us, she hugged me and burst into tears. We realized then that she had an injury below her chin and had to be stitched up. That was our Unnati—who put up a brave front before others, but was a little baby with her parents, wanting, like any other child, to only be pampered and cajoled.

Four years later, we were blessed with a son. We decided to call him 'Ujjwal', which means brightness, but at home, he was Ujju to us. Born with congenital lactose intolerance, he was allergic to any kind of milk or milk products. This condition is caused by lactase deficiency, or hypolactasia. Congenital lactase deficiency prevents babies from feeding on even their mother's milk. Ujjwal was diagnosed with this, but he responded well to the treatment. At that time, there was no substitute for milk, so I was advised by the paediatrician to prepare soya feed for him. I used to prepare his feed twenty-four hours in advance and then refrigerate it. Being a lactose intolerant child, he was also plagued by other medical issues, but we were careful and vigilant. I remember distinctly that during his first year, we spent a lot of time with doctors, but finally, we managed to pull him out of this phase of poor health.

Unfortunately, a little later he developed bronchial asthma. The attacks were very severe and frequent, and at times we had to rush him to the hospital in the middle of the night. He was on antibiotics and steroids for a long period of time, and this was a cause of great concern for us. We were advised to get a nebulizer for him, which, at that time, was not available in India. However, since Shekhar often travelled overseas, he was able to get one and this helped Ujjwal immensely.

On the advice of a family friend, we took Ujjwal to Hyderabad for the fish treatment administered by the Bathini Goud brothers. He responded favourably to the treatment, and fortunately, the intensity and frequency of the attacks decreased.

At the age of four, Ujjwal was admitted to Delhi Public School, Mathura Road. Like Unnati, he was very fond of going to school. An intelligent child, he became a scholar badge holder. But, like any other child, he was extremely naughty. He loved music and we encouraged him to train in Hindustani classical music. He was very fond of playing cricket and would never miss an opportunity to watch matches. Once, we had all gone to watch the Mithun Chakraborty starrer *Disco Dancer* at Uphaar. As soon as the hit song 'I am a Disco Dancer' began, both children started dancing to the song! The other moviegoers were so amused that they all started looking at Ujjwal and Unnati, rather than watching what was happening on screen.

Ujjwal was one of the lead singers in the western music band in his school. He always said that his most memorable moment was when he sang his first ad jingle standing on a stool, because he was too short to reach the mic. They were both very fond of watching movies and it was this love for movies that led to their untimely deaths. As long as we live, we will regret the day we booked those tickets for them.

Both Unnati and Ujjwal were good students and we never received any complaints about them from their school. Both were very outgoing and had many friends. Both our children were very attached to one another, but like siblings are wont to do, they would often get into fights as well. As a mother, I often had to intervene, and the one strategy that always worked was when I asked them to sit in separate rooms and not speak to each other. It was impossible for them to not talk to one another and within a matter of minutes, they would apologize and promise not to repeat their mistake. Naturally, being children, the promise was rarely kept.

The siblings were also very different in many ways. While Ujjwal loved the fun, frolic and colour associated with Holi and the crackers of Diwali, Unnati was always terrified of them and steered clear of both. How were we to know that perhaps her fear of fire would turn into a nightmare for all of us?

We felt a deep sense of content and could not have asked for more from life. We soon opened our own garment export business, which demanded a lot of travel. While Shekhar travelled, I held the fort in Delhi and took care of the children, house and the business here.

We often planned vacations with the children. We would drive up to the hills in Shimla and thereabouts. Since work demanded that Shekhar remain in Chennai for prolonged periods of time, we would join him there for long vacations.

Shekhar started singing professionally in the 1980s, when he was invited to record with T-series. Later, he went on to lend his voice to a lot of commercial jingles in different languages, for a variety of products and also recorded the title songs for many television serials. He performed live in India and overseas, with shows in Holland and Spain, among other countries. Since both children were learning music and were good singers, they too lent their voices for commercial jingles. However, despite his unmistakable gift for it, music remained only a hobby for Shekhar.

On one occasion, Shekhar was performing for a popular television channel and both kids were part of the audience. The producer of the show approached me, asking if Ujjwal could be cast as an actor for a forthcoming TV serial. I turned down the offer as I did not want him to be distracted from his studies. But, at the same time, I promised Ujjwal that I would produce a music album for him once he finished school. Life did not give me the chance to fulfil my promise.

The month of July always reminds us of the time both the kids suffered major health problems. On 7 July 1992, when Ujjwal was barely nine years old, when he was getting ready to go to school, I realized that he had a high temperature and decided to keep him at home that day. Around noon, he started vomiting and developed pain in his abdomen. Without losing time, we rushed him to a paediatrician, who advised us to get certain blood tests carried out on Ujjwal. Since he did not have a lab attached to his clinic, we had to get the test done in a lab in Panchsheel Park. It started raining heavily and the roads were waterlogged.

We managed to reach the lab with a great deal of difficulty. We got the reports that evening and we decided to get a second opinion. The other doctor confirmed that Ujjwal was suffering from acute appendicitis and advised surgery. We contacted a surgeon and admitted Ujjwal to a hospital. The surgery started around midnight. While we were waiting for him to be wheeled into the operation theatre, Ujjwal saw the tense looks on our faces. He smiled at us and told us not to worry as he would be fine. The surgery was successful and he recovered quickly, and was able to go to school again.

Three years later, on 14 July 1995, Unnati woke me up early in the morning and complained that she was experiencing acute abdominal pain. Unfortunately the landline phone was not working that day and there were no mobile phones at that time. I woke my neighbour up and called my doctor. He asked me to rush her to the hospital without wasting any more time. The doctor, after examining her, said she needed to undergo a blood test. She too was diagnosed with acute appendicitis and had to undergo surgery. Since Unnati had seen Ujjwal going through the whole process, she was not nervous. However, as parents, we were anxious. Fortunately for us, the surgery was successful. Ironically, both kids were operated by the same surgeon at the same hospital—three years apart.

Unnati and Ujjwal were both born in August, and as a result, it was a month of celebrations and partying for the family. Birthday parties were always eagerly planned and anticipated. And with many friends and family members to celebrate with, the kids always ended up having multiple parties, blowing the candles on a number of cakes. There would always be one cake for friends, another for the family and yet another if the need arose!

In 1996, Unnati had gone out with her friends to celebrate her birthday during the day, while we had family and friends over for dinner. When she came home at 11 p.m., I told her that I was glad she had returned in time to cut her cake with us. She responded by saying lightly that the next year we would have to cut the cake ourselves with just her photograph placed in front, because by then she would have turned eighteen and would be off to a disco with her friends.

We would have never suspected then that what she said would turn out to be tragically and devastatingly true.

In November 1996, Ujjwal came back home from school with his right arm swollen. He also complained that it hurt a lot. On being questioned, he was very evasive and did not tell me what exactly had happened. I decided to take him to an orthopaedic surgeon. When the doctor asked him how he managed to fracture his arm, he told him that he had been part of a brawl in school. While casting a plaster on his arm, the doctor sympathized with him, but said that Ujjwal would not be able to burst crackers on Diwali—something he looked forward to every year. Ujjwal very promptly replied that being left-handed, he would not let the plaster dampen the spirit of the festival. True to his words, he burst a lot of crackers that year, despite the cast on his arm. Little did we realize that this was his last Diwali.

Ujjwal always loved watching movies on television. He also disliked any disturbance and hated answering the phone and the doorbell when he watched a movie. In May 1997, a mere month before he was snatched away from us, he was alone at home watching a film when the doorbell rang. It was a delivery boy, who had come to deliver a bouquet of flowers for Unnati. He accepted it and kept it aside. Fifteen minutes later the bell rang again and the same delivery boy was there with another bouquet. When the doorbell rang for the third time, he asked the delivery boy how many more bouquets he was supposed to deliver. He was informed that he had been instructed to deliver twelve bouquets at intervals of fifteen minutes. An exasperated Ujjwal told the boy to deliver all the bouquets at one go, assuring him that he would inform Unnati that they were delivered at intervals of fifteen minutes. When both of us and Unnati reached home, the drawing room was full of Dutch roses and we all had a hearty laugh as we tried to figure out who this mysterious admirer of Unnati was.

In 1997, Ujjwal was promoted to class nine and he decided to pursue his studies as a marine engineer. Unnati had appeared for the class twelve board exams. We were very anxious about Unnati's results, though she had never given us any reason to worry. When on 30 May, the results were declared, we were hugely relieved to learn that Unnati had performed very well. It was time for her to make a decision about her career and she chose to become a Company Secretary. We helped her enrol as a student at the Institute of Company Secretaries, but she also wanted to do a B.Com Honours course simultaneously at one of the colleges under the Delhi University. She filled the admission forms and I requested a member of my staff to submit them since I did not want Unnati to go through the rigmarole of going from one college to another. We had promised both the children that once Unnati's forms were submitted, we would all go on a vacation. But that was not to be . . .

Our children loved presenting us with greeting cards on every occasion, big or small. The day Unnati received her examination results, she presented us with a loving thank you card, signed 'Niti Baba'. The message read: 'I am glad you're my parents, I see a reflection of you in all my accomplishments, your support and love always guide me, so much of who I am, I owe to you. No matter where my life may take me, a part of you will always be with me. I can't thank you enough for all you have given me and done for me, I couldn't have asked for more loving and special parents. You are the best.'

It was the last card we would receive from her. In their absence, Shekhar and I often look through the carefully preserved cards the children presented us. Even today, they continue to speak to us, through the many messages full of love and laughter that ceased abruptly on 13 June 1997.

2

Tragedy Strikes

In 1997, we had reached that wonderful point where we were behaving less like parents with our children and more like friends. We always encouraged them to talk openly about everything and guided them only when we felt there was a need to do so. They were wonderful children and we were immensely proud of them. Even today, though we have had to live without them for nineteen years now, we take comfort in the fact that they loved us and made us very proud.

What isn't easy to forget is how quickly it all fell apart, just a few months later.

It was summer vacation time and the children had planned to go watch a movie. They were very excited about watching the much-awaited and controversial new movie *Border*.

The tragic day started off normally. Unnati asked me to book tickets for the matinee show of *Border* on the day it hit theatres. We told her that we could all go together later that day, but she insisted on going for the matinee show. We booked their tickets and we live with that guilt to this day.

Since my brother-in-law was in hospital recovering from bypass surgery, I had to rush there early every morning to relieve my sister. I had made lunch for the children before heading to the hospital. It was too early to buy chicken from the market, so I prepared the basic sauce for the curry and asked Shekhar to have the chicken delivered to our home. I instructed him to add the sauce, top it with some soya sauce and cook the dish for twenty minutes.

When Shekhar came back from the gym, he followed my instructions and asked Unnati if she knew how much soya sauce I added when cooking chicken. Since my daughter had little or no interest in cooking, she too had no idea of the recipe and the proportions. Between father and daughter, they decided to add the soya sauce as per their judgment. This was the first time Shekhar had made the dish, not realizing that the children were destined to have their last meal cooked by him.

Excited as they always were at the thought of watching a much-awaited movie, the kids kissed us, said their byes and left.

A little while later, we also left to our office in Malviya Nagar. We were at work till 7 p.m., completely unaware of the fire at the cinema hall. We left to check on Yogesh, my brother-in-law. At around 7.30 p.m., I called the house to check on the children, but there was no response. We paged Unnati and waited for fifteen minutes for her to respond or call us back as she normally did. We grew increasingly anxious when there was no response and repeatedly called the phone at home. We also sent several messages on Unnati's pager saying, 'Getting worried call back on mobile.' Alas, there was no response.

We rushed home to check if the kids had returned, but they hadn't. Not imagining anything dangerous had happened to them, I told Shekhar that they must have gone to buy a card and gift for him as the next day was Father's Day. The house was in darkness and I quickly went to my puja room and lit a lamp. I prayed to god, asking for the well-being of our children. Shekhar stood outside on the balcony, anxiously waiting for them to return.

By now, we were desperately worried. I called up Uphaar Cinema, but I could not get through to their number. I also called up AIIMS to check if any mishap had occurred, but that number didn't go through either. Just then, Vishal, one of Unnati's friends, called and we asked him if he had spoken to Unnati. When I told him that I was extremely worried as she had gone to watch a movie and had not yet returned, he quickly asked me which theatre she had gone to. When I mentioned Uphaar, he choked.

It was Vishal who informed us that there had been a major fire in Uphaar Cinema. He told us that there had been only seven casualties. We prayed silently, hoping that our children were not among them.

We rushed to Uphaar with Vishal, and on the way, we called friends and family and informed them of the fire and asked them to go to AIIMS and Safdarjung Hospital to help us locate the kids. On reaching the area, we found that Uphaar had been cordoned off and were told by the police that we should make our inquiries at AIIMS, situated less than a kilometre from the cinema hall.

The enormity of the situation sank in only after we reached AIIMS. The roads were blocked with cars and scores of people were milling around, adding to the chaos. We could hear them screaming and shouting. We left our car on the main road and rushed into the hospital.

Outside the casualty ward, I asked Vishal to check the list of the injured, but the names of our children were not on it. Nonetheless, we started looking for them among the injured. I asked Shekhar to walk across the road to Safdarjung Hospital to check if they had been admitted there. As I was talking to Shekhar, a lady, who I presume was a social worker, asked me how old my children were and, on hearing my response, she took us to the OPD block.

As we entered the OPD block, we saw bodies lined up on stretchers. I recognized Unnati from the churidar–kurta she had been wearing that day. Her body was the second one in the row.

We rushed towards her, but she lay there, cold and motionless. Unable to believe my eyes, I fainted. Once I regained consciousness, I asked Shekhar about Ujjwal. He told me that Ujjwal had not survived the fire either. His body lay just two stretchers away from Unnati's. Both of them had identification numbers pasted on their foreheads.

The news devastated me. I remember vividly that by that time, most of our relatives and friends had reached AIIMS. I was too shocked by everything that transpired then, but I do remember that the hospital authorities decided to release the dead bodies to relatives without conducting post-mortems. The decision was probably taken by the lieutenant governor of Delhi, keeping in mind the volatility of the situation. The crowded corridors of the hospital were reverberating with the shrieks and wails of family members who had gathered there in the hope of finding their loved ones safe.

The world had come to an end for us. We could not believe that Unnati and Ujjwal, who had left the house to watch a movie, were no more. Instead of greeting them warmly and asking them how the movie was, we were going back home with their bodies. We were cursing ourselves for having bought the tickets to death for our children. We tried desperately to grapple with the many thoughts that flooded our minds. How many times might they have called out for us in their last moments? Were they together when the fire broke out? How much had they suffered? Did Ujjwal pass away first or did Unnati? Did Ujjwal have time to even try and use his inhaler? Were they together when the smoke overwhelmed them?

We have not found the answers to these questions till today.

We collected their bodies from AIIMS, the same hospital from which we had, as proud parents, brought them home as babies.

All I can remember is that when we reached home, we found that somebody had cleared the drawing room of the furniture and carpet, and Unnati and Ujjwal were lying there on blocks of ice. I could not bear to see my children, who had always hated sleeping on the floor, lying there. It seemed insensitive to place them on the ground, but where else was I supposed to move them? It was in this very room that we had shared so many special moments. It was here that we had lived through the happy times and laughter. It was in this room that we had celebrated their birthdays and watched them grow up. This room was now witness to their eternal silence.

I sat next to my children through the night, hoping for a miracle that would wake them up, hoping to hear them say, 'Mom, we are back!' I know now that I was in a state of denial. It was only in the morning when our relatives asked us to perform their last rites that I realized it was not a bad dream, but our horrific reality.

By the next morning, a lot of people had come home. My sister, who was with her husband in hospital, was told of our loss early that morning by her in-laws. Yogesh also heard from the hospital staff about the fire at Uphaar Cinema. When he did not see me in hospital that morning, he became a little suspicious. He was aware that Unnati was fond of watching movies; he was concerned that the children might have been involved in the mishap. His doctors advised us not to break the news to him, since he had recently undergone bypass surgery. But my sister told me that Yogesh was insisting on speaking to me, to be assured that all was well. It took a lot of courage for me to hold myself together and to tell him that the children were fine. But once that was done, I broke down completely; it was very traumatic for me to pretend they were okay, considering they lay dead before my eyes. I realize that it had to be done. After all, we did not want another casualty in the family.

I was in for more shocks that morning, as I bathed my children in accordance with Hindu rituals. There were bruises around Unnati and Ujjwal's necks, caused by someone who had snatched the gold chains from their bodies. Unnati's earlobe had been torn as somebody had tried to pull her earrings off too and Ujjwal's watch was missing. I was stunned—even at a time of tragedy, greed and the lure of gold had left indelible scars on them. What faith could I repose in humanity, in the face of scavengers who had treated the bodies of my children thus?

But not all was gone. I found Ujjwal's wallet in his jeans. It held the tickets to the show; tickets we have preserved till today.

The image of my children's pyre haunts me till date. I have never been able to get this out of my mind. When their pyres were lit, I felt pain sear through me. I knew I would never be able to discard this image from my mind and had told Shekhar's family I preferred my children be taken to the electric crematorium. Sadly, my request was not heeded.

Shekhar's family took all the decisions and Shekhar was denied the right to perform the last rites for Unnati, because the family insisted that as per their customs and traditions, a father cannot perform the last rites for both children at the same time. It was his elder brother who lit Unnati's pyre and this is one decision we still regret. Shekhar was too traumatized to insist on doing it himself. How we wish that the family had respected our decisions, rather than imposing their customs and traditions on us!

Our faith in god died forever on 13 June 1997, the day we lost our children. That was the last day we lit a lamp in front of the idol at home. We decided never to pray to him again, because it would no longer make any difference to us. What should we pray for? When our children had been alive, we would take them to Tirupati, Vaishno Devi, Kanyakumari and other religious places. None of those trips seemed to hold meaning any more.

Now, we do not believe in any divine power. When our children died, we were left with two choices, both equally harsh—either to sit back, cry and accept what had taken place as fate or fight for justice. We chose the latter. We did not want to blame destiny for the blows it had dealt us. If at all god exists, why would he want so many people to die in such a brutal way? That was when we made a promise to our children and to ourselves. We would seek punishment for those who were responsible for their deaths.

After we immersed the children's ashes in Haridwar, one of our relatives suggested that we move forward with our lives. She went to the extent of suggesting that we start a family all over again. We were aghast at this insensitive suggestion. Over the years, many of our friends and relatives have suggested adopting a child, but we could never bring ourselves to even consider the thought. We knew that if we did so, the child would always have to live under the shadow of our grief and he/she would probably hate us for this.

While condoling our loss, people try to console us by saying that life goes on. They are wrong, because only those who go through the pain of loss know that it never passes. We feel as though we have been served a death sentence, even though we are still living.

Shekhar and I made a conscious decision to stay focused on our mission to ensure our children get justice. We told our families not to interfere with this and to respect our feelings. The family was against our decision to fight the Ansals, the influential owners of the cinema hall, and the rest of the system to get justice. Everyone who mattered told us that it was not possible to fight such a powerful builder lobby. We were told time and again that money, muscle and political contacts could bring our efforts to naught.

But nothing would deter us. We were determined not to spare the killers of our children, no matter how powerful they may be. We knew we would fight till the end.

3

Coping

There can be no greater sorrow for parents than to witness the death of their children. We experienced intense anger, disbelief, guilt, denial, sorrow and fear—all of it affecting us in turns. We often felt hopeless and isolated, and it took a toll on both of us. Our lives had changed forever and, until today, we cannot say we have gotten over the grief. It has been very difficult for us to smile, laugh and find joy again. We always looked for the smallest reasons to celebrate, but now, it is impossible to find a single reason to smile.

After the ceremonies on the thirteenth day concluded, when everybody went back to their lives, the two of us were left alone. We quickly realized that we only had each other for support. As time passed, we also realized that it was not possible for us to talk about our children to others because they would just look the other way and not want to listen to what we had to say. Perhaps they did not know how to react, or were frightened at the prospect of such a loss, or were just awkward when it came to expressing their feelings. We decided we would talk about the children only between ourselves.

We have no legacy to leave behind and as we grow older, there is no one to take care of us. We have no moral or social support. We often wonder who will perform the last rites for us when our time comes. The pain continues to haunt us.

In the beginning, I suffered from a form of insomnia. When I did go to sleep with the help of three or four sedatives, I would do so hoping that I would not have to wake up to this cruel world again. In the dead of night, I would go into the kids' room hoping to sense their presence there. We have left everything intact: their books, soft toys, clothes, Ujjwal's cricket set and a cap he was very fond of. He had left it on his pillow, not knowing that he would never wear it again. In the early years, I would often switch on the AC at night, only to remember later that they were deep in slumber elsewhere.

Shekhar and I used to be fitness freaks and we would spend an hour in the gym every day before going to work, but we stopped going due to our state of acute depression. As a result, this took a toll on my health and I started suffering from headaches and breathing problems. My physician diagnosed it as hypertension. I also developed acute cervical spondylitis due to stress and depression. I was not responding to any painkillers and was advised physiotherapy, but nothing gave me any relief.

In October 2001, around the time the hearing for our civil matter was scheduled, I was becoming more and more concerned about how Shekhar would manage on his own if I was unable to attend the hearings due to my health issues. I sought medical advice and learnt that the only option available was to undergo the painful and risky process of having steroids injected between my cervical discs. The potential risk of this process causing irrevocable nerve damage was also explained to me in no uncertain terms. But I insisted that I would undergo the treatment at my own peril. Shekhar did not agree with me and was very reluctant about my decision to go ahead, and asked me to continue physiotherapy for some more time, but I refused to listen to him. I knew I was taking a big risk that could potentially lead to multiple complications, but I still took the chance— just so that I could attend the court sessions to brief my counsel. Fortunately for me, the treatment helped.

I used to be very fond of cooking, and both Unnati and Ujjwal enjoyed the food I made for them. Despite my busy schedule, I would take time out to cook and ensure that both Shekhar and I were home to have lunch with the children. But now, food and eating meals on time are no longer a priority for either of us. We live on coffee and tea, and if at all we are hungry, we eat some junk food. We avoid eating out, knowing fully well that seeing a family enjoying a meal together at a restaurant will always bring back painful memories for us.

Both of us enjoyed socializing with friends and relatives, and would never miss an opportunity to attend the weddings we were invited to. But after the tragedy, we have not attended even one wedding in the family, for the sole reason that we are reminded, yet again, that we will never have the opportunity to watch our children get married. We cannot even imagine what they would have looked like as a bride and a groom.

We could never have imagined life without our children and yet, we have been forced to live without them for so many years. Though we saw many ups and downs in our business, we were never deterred in our pursuit of success.

I used to always tell Shekhar it was just a bad phase that we would overcome, which would only help our business grow. But this loss is one we cannot reconcile ourselves to. We have lost interest in all material things and, as a result, our business took a back seat in our lives. Both of us had worked very hard to establish it so that we could provide the best for our children. We were on the verge of diversifying and starting an editing studio, for which we had made huge investments. But none of this was to be. The tragedy left us completely shattered. We decided to drop the idea of setting up the editing studio, despite the investments. Our garment business required a lot of travelling and demanded our time, but it was not possible for either of us to leave the other alone in Delhi. Hence, we decided to limit our work to those areas that did not require travelling, as it was important for us to remain in Delhi and follow our case.

We often asked ourselves what we were saving our money for, when we could not spend it on our children. We had given them good lives. We had looked forward to a bright future for them, but our dreams were shattered due to the greed of the cinema owners, who wanted to give their family the best, over the dead bodies of our children.

Over time we also learnt that some people cannot speak compassionately to bereaved parents. What many believe to be a comforting statement is most often not. People have told us that time is a healer, that we should move on with life and that whatever happens, happens for the greater good. They do not realize that the loss of a child is a wound that never heals completely and that living without your children is like living with a wound that bleeds forever. How can bereaved parents move on with their lives when they have lost their most precious treasure? The only things we hold on to are the memories of our children and our love for them. By doing so, we are moving forward, but we never really move on.

When someone tells us that whatever happens, happens for the greater good, it makes our blood boil. This is sheer insensitivity! How can there be any good in children dying before their parents? Such unsolicited advice and platitudes offer no comfort to us. One of the comments that enraged us most was when a person equated her grief over losing a dog to our loss, and said that she understood what it means to lose children.

We have also come to realize that we Indians do not know how to handle grief. Friends and relatives feel that by visiting once or by being present at the cremation and the prayer meeting, their obligations are over. There is no emotional support to handle the terrible loneliness and anguish one feels. What one needs is true compassion and companionship, not mere formal expressions of sympathy and condolence. When it is time to party, there is no dearth of friends and relatives to party with you, but when you grieve, you grieve alone. We feel horribly let down by our friends and relatives. It is unacceptable how people change overnight. In our case, they began to treat us as though we were socially untouchable.

The pain of losing your children is like no other kind of pain you encounter in your life. Parents are not prepared to deal with this loss at all. We often sit and wonder what word should parents who lose their children be called, but there is no word for it. When a man loses his wife, he is called a widower; when a woman loses her spouse, she is a widow. When children lose their parents, they are called orphans. But in this case, perhaps no word can encompass the sheer pain felt.

Each year, the death anniversary of our children drains us emotionally. The grief continues unabated. They have left such a huge void in our lives and there is the sense of so much potential that has not been realized. Our children would have been in their thirties now had they lived, and possibly, married. We may even have been grandparents by now.

These gaping wounds neither heal nor cease to hurt. Our children are gone forever and we will never get to hug them again or tell them how much we love them. There will never be closure for us, and we will have to labour through life carrying the scars and the intense pain with us.

Not a single day passes without us thinking about Unnati and Ujjwal. We love them and will miss them for as long as we live. Nineteen years later and it still feels like yesterday! There are times when the pain is so intense that we are unable to talk and all we can do is break down completely. No one can truly understand our pain.

4

How Entertainment Turned into Death

Uphaar Cinema, one of the best-known stand-alone theatres in Delhi, was located in Green Park Extension, a posh area in south Delhi. The cinema hall, constructed in 1973, had four storeys. Its auditorium had a sanctioned capacity of 750 seats and the balcony had a sanctioned capacity of 250 seats. The auditorium was situated on the first floor of the cinema, while the balcony was constructed on the mezzanine floor. The ground floor of the building housed a parking lot in addition to three separate rooms on the western side, one of which had a 500 KVA transformer inside that supplied electricity to the theatre. The second room was used to house a 1000 KVA transformer that was installed by the Delhi Vidyut Board (DVB) to supply electricity to some tenants in the commercial complex that formed a part of the cinema building, as well as to other consumers in the locality. The third room housed high tension panels, low tension panels, battery chargers and a metering cubicle belonging to the Delhi Vidyut Board.

As per available records of Delhi Vidyut Board and the Delhi Fire Service, a fire broke out at 6.55 a.m. on the morning of 13 June 1997. It started in the DVB transformer installed in the ground floor car parking area. The fire was brought under control by about 7.25 a.m. The DVB staff carried out repairs and electricity was restored to the cinema by 11.30 a.m.

That Friday, the film *Border* was released. It was based on the events of the 1971 Indo–Pak war. Enthusiastic moviegoers thronged the cinema hall, oblivious to the horror they would encounter in the next two hours. There was uninterrupted power supply until 3.55 p.m. and all was well until the interval.

There was scheduled load shedding from 3.55 to 4.55 p.m. After the interval, when the electricity was restored around 4.55 p.m., there was heavy arcing and sparking in the B phase of the DVB transformer. This resulted in one of the cables of the transformer becoming loose, which eventually came off and dangled along the radiator. It burnt a hole in the radiator through which transformer oil started leaking out. On account of the heat generated by the loose cable touching the radiator, it caught fire. A loud sound was heard from the substation and oil from the transformer started spilling on the floor of the DVB transformer room. The fire quickly spread into the parking lot and came in contact with a Contessa car parked right outside and, as a result, the cars parked on the ground floor of the cinema hall were set ablaze.

Thick smoke from the parking lot started billowing in the north and southward direction. As the smoke rose up the stairwell, due to a chimney effect, it entered the auditorium through the door and AC duct. The smoke billowing southwards travelled up through another staircase into the lower portion of the balcony. The 750 patrons sitting in the first floor of the auditorium escaped immediately thanks to the properly spaced exits. The staff in the basement and the tenants on the ground floor, those closest to the fire, along with those in the third and fourth floor, all escaped.

But as smoke and carbon monoxide engulfed the balcony, the patrons began to suffocate and there was complete pandemonium. Despite the fact that a fire had broken out, the projector operator was not instructed to stop the film; neither were the patrons informed of the accident nor were they given instructions on how to leave the auditorium and the balcony. When the electricity failed completely it became even more difficult for those in the balcony to make their way out. Emergency lights were non-functional and there were no exit signs. Even the public address system, which is mandatory in a cinema hall, was not working. Moreover, the exit on the right side was closed in order to accommodate a private box for the owners. With one gangway closed completely and one more made narrower to accommodate extra seats, there was not enough space for everyone to leave. The gatekeeper had also bolted the doors of the balcony during the movie—all of this only ensured that the people in the balcony were completely trapped. With the carbon monoxide and smoke leaking into the balcony, it resembled a gas chamber.

Unnati and Ujjwal were seated in seats A-4 and A-5 on the right side of the balcony. Had the exit next to them and the gangway not been blocked, our children could have walked out to safety and would have been alive today. But the management did not provide sufficient passage for free movement as required under the provisions of law and therefore, perpetrated this dreadful incident.

The patrons who escaped from the balcony had harrowing tales to tell. According to them, soon after the song 'Sandese Aate Hain' finished, the viewers saw smoke rising up from the left side of the screen. There was an explosion, followed by cries warning of fire. Looking down from the balcony, they saw that the auditorium was empty. The movie stopped playing at 5.05 p.m., only because the main power supply tripped from the AIIMS grid. There was thick black smoke curling through the theatre.

Panic gripped the people. There was no announcement system, no emergency lights, no gatekeeper, no ushers with torches and it was pitch-dark inside. There was no help from the management. There was commotion in the balcony as all the doors were bolted and the moviegoers started to feel suffocated. Some fell unconscious then and there, and succumbed to the poisonous gas.

Those who managed to wrench the middle door of the balcony open came into the lobby, which was also full of smoke. Moreover, the glass door leading to the staircase on the right had also been bolted. In the ensuing melee, people coughed, choked and gasped for air.

Finally, the door to the staircase was forced open. Since the staircase was also full of the black, toxic smoke, people could not use it. As people tried to move towards the terrace, they encountered lot of obstructions due to unauthorized construction carried out by the owners of the hall. The door leading to the terrace was also locked, and the patrons stuck on the fourth floor had to come down with the help of ropes and a hydraulic lift provided by fire officials. Some of them managed to break the windowpane and jump from the second floor. They were grievously injured in the process.

Some took shelter in the toilets and eventually died due to asphyxia.

The fire broke out at 4.55 p.m. The first call to the Delhi Fire Service was made at 5.10 p.m. by the deputy general manager of the cinema—fifteen minutes after the fire erupted. Had the management not wasted those precious fifteen minutes, the lives of the innocent patrons might have been saved.

The first fire officer reached the hall at 5.21 p.m. The fire was declared as 'serious' at 5.50 p.m. It had been brought under control by 6.20 p.m. It was only after this that the rescue operation began.

According to the officers who took part in the rescue operations, visibility was extremely poor; so much so, they could not even see each other when they entered the cinema. Delhi Fire Services (DFS) officers rescued the people trapped in the balcony by opening the bolted doors and taking those who had collapsed and those who had been injured to hospitals nearby. No one from the staff or management of the cinema hall was present to lend a helping hand. According to DFS officials, most of the casualties were reported in the balcony, the toilets, the lobby outside the balcony and the adjoining offices.

Since only one ambulance was available at the location, most of the injured and unconscious people were transported to AIIMS and Safdarjung Hospital via private vehicles, Sub-Divisional Magistrate's vehicles, PCR vans and local tempos. It is a matter of good fortune that two big and important hospitals, AIIMS and Safdarjung, were located near Uphaar, resulting in most of the unconscious and injured persons being taken there within a short span of time.

5

Those Who Suffered

This incident resulted in the loss of fifty-nine precious human lives and left over a hundred people injured. It ruined twenty-eight families. The youngest to succumb to the fire was a one-month-old girl named Chetna and the oldest was a seventy-two-year-old man Kartar K. Malhotra. Each family continues to live with the trauma of losing loved ones. Each family has a harrowing tale to tell.

Satya Pal Sudan lost seven members of his family, including his granddaughter, Chetna. He received a call and was told that there had been a fire at Uphaar Cinema. He rushed to the spot, only to find that his entire family had been snatched away from him. Sudan recalls that when he saw his granddaughter's body still cuddled to her mother's, not only he, but the doctors and policemen at the AIIMS mortuary were also in tears. He did not have enough space in his house to keep all the dead bodies, and hence took them to the cremation ground directly from the mortuary. Sudan, who is seventy-four years old today, has nobody to look after him and his wife.

They have no desire to live any more.

Vikas lost his father, Kishanlal, who used to own a small shop and was the sole breadwinner for the family. Vikas was sixteen when disaster struck and had wanted to study further; but now he had to shoulder responsibility for his family—his mother and five siblings. His life changed and his dreams were shattered. Despite the fact he suffers from epilepsy, he runs a small catering business to make ends meet.

Naveen Sawhney, seventy, lost his only daughter, Tarika, to the fire. She was twenty-one and was pursuing her studies at Jesus and Mary College under the Delhi University. A very loving and friendly young woman, she was looking forward to a family vacation in Goa later in June. In fact, she had gone to her college that day to get her concession form signed for her air ticket. Along with her friend Ruby, she decided to go for the matinee show of *Border* at Uphaar. Since the manager of the theatre was an acquaintance of her father's, Tarika called him up and booked the tickets. Unfortunately, both Tarika and Ruby passed away. Life changed overnight for the Sawhneys, who were planning for Tarika's wedding at the end of the year. She was to settle down in the USA after her marriage. Today, the Sawhneys miss her and cherish the memories of all the good times they shared with her.

13 June 1997 was Mohan Lal Sehgal's fiftieth birthday, a day to celebrate and treasure the memories of a lifetime with his family, but it turned into the darkest day of his life. No one could have imagined that the entire family would meet later in the day to mourn the death of his son Vikas Sehgal. He still rues the fact that he gave Vikas the money to watch the film that fateful day. His son was preparing for his National Defence Academy examination and had

he survived, in just six more days he would have turned twenty-one. Almost nineteen years have passed since the fire, but there has not been even a single moment when the Sehgals don't remember their son.

R.S. Rahi's son Sudeep was the youngest among his three children. He was studying hotel management and was in Delhi for the summer. His birthday was the next day, 14 June, and he planned to go shopping with his elder brother. Instead, he changed his mind and decided to accompany his friends to the movie. Unfortunately, Sudeep had to be cremated on 14 June at 2.45 p.m.—on the same date and time he was born. Rahi passed away in January 2016, still waiting to get justice for his son.

Kanwaljeet Bhalla is haunted by the fact that it was at her insistence that her husband agreed to watch *Border* that fateful day. Ironically, except for her husband, Captain I.S. Bhalla, everyone who went with her survived. Kanwaljeet still maintains that it is tragic that her husband came home unharmed from the 1965 war, but died watching a film based on the 1971 war with Pakistan.

Nanak Chand who is seventy-nine years old today lost his twenty-nine-year-old son Yash Pal, who was the youngest among five siblings. Yash Pal was a dentist by profession and was engaged, with the wedding scheduled for later that year. He had gone to watch the movie along with his friends. Destiny has been exceptionally cruel to Nanak Chand—in 2003, his older son Raj Kumar, then aged thirty-seven, died in an accident. Today, both Nanak Chand and his wife suffer from depression.

Durga Dass lost his eighteen-year-old son Ravi, the youngest among his children. Still studying in school, he had gone alone to watch the film and was among the fifty-nine in the balcony who lost their lives. Durga Dass lost his wife in 2015 and he too passed away in February 2016, awaiting justice for his son.

Nedup Wangyal and Kunga Wangyal were aged eighteen and fourteen respectively at the time of the Uphaar Cinema fire. Their father, Pema Wangyal, aged forty-four, was an income tax officer for the government of Sikkim and their mother, Pema Namgyal, aged forty-three, was a school teacher at Tashi Namgyal Academy. They were in Delhi to help their elder son secure admission in a college, but perished in the fire. Nedup and Kunga were taken care of by relatives, but there isn't a moment when they don't think of their parents. Though they are constantly pained by the fact that they were robbed of seeing their parents age gracefully, they are grateful to their parents for giving them so much strength. They could not spend much time with their parents, but the little time they had was not wasted. There isn't a single day that goes by when they don't miss their parents, and the siblings frequently wonder how different life would have been if they were still alive.

The Kapurs can never forget the last memory of their twenty-one-year-old daughter Ruby waving to them as they left for a pilgrimage to Vaishno Devi on 13 June 1997. Ruby had decided to stay back with her grandmother for her college examinations. She decided to watch the movie with her friend Tarika, but they never returned. Ruby's mother, Nilu, still regrets leaving her behind in Delhi. Her brother, Gobind, who was ten years old in 1997, remembers her as a very cheerful and helpful person. She was engaged to be married soon. Every year starts off with a grim reminder of Ruby's absence—she was born on 1 January. They all wish her a happy birthday, hoping that wherever she is their wishes reach her. Not a single day goes by when they do not remember her or miss her.

Captain Vardip Singh Bhinder, aged eighty-five, lost his son, Captain Manjinder Singh Bhinder, who was twenty-nine years old then, his daughter-in-law, Jotroop Kaur, who was twenty-seven years old at the time of the tragedy, and his four-year-old grandson, Ruskin Bhinder. Captain Manjinder Bhinder was the best rider in the country. Today his father is virtually blind and bedridden. His mother, aged seventy-two, faces great difficulty moving around because both her knees are severely affected by arthritis. They are dependent on their three daughters to take care of them.

Maheshwari Devi had gone to watch the film with her husband, her son, two daughters and her nephew. She lost both her husband, P.C. Gupta, aged forty-two, and her son Ajay, who was sixteen in 1997 and was a student of class ten, to the fire. Maheshwari Devi was a housewife, so the responsibility of running the family's garment business and ensuring the two sisters got married fell on the shoulders of her older son, Rakesh. The incident has left an indelible scar on the family. Today, like other members of Association of Victims of Uphaar Fire Tragedy (AVUT), the Gupta family is awaiting justice.

6

Preparing for Battle

Through the haze of our pain, we learnt from newspapers that the state government had ordered an inquiry into the cause of the Uphaar fire and appointed the deputy commissioner (south) to file a report by the first week of July.

After performing the thirteenth day rituals for our children, Shekhar and I went through each and every paper that came out on 14 June, and then every single day after that, to try and figure out what exactly happened. As per the reports, the fire originated at the DVB transformer, which had been installed on the ground floor of the cinema hall. The smoke had entered the auditorium and the balcony through AC ducts and other vulnerable points. It was also reported that the deaths and injuries occurred only in the balcony, as the exits and gangways had been blocked by additional seats that were installed—a clear violation of the rules.

We were obsessed with finding out whether our children had been carried out of the cinema hall alive and if their lives could have been saved. To do so, we needed to obtain the video footage shot at the scene that tragic day by the media. We decided to approach different television channels, asking them to share their footage from 13 June 1997. The media persons we approached were very compassionate and readily agreed to give us the raw footage shot by their teams covering the tragedy. It took us unimaginable courage to view these videos. The visuals were very disturbing, but we went through all of the footage with a fine-toothed comb. Unfortunately, we could not locate our children in any of it. However, one visual disturbed us immensely: The manager of Uphaar, standing outside the hall, dressed in spotless white, clutching a black bag that presumably held the day's collection from the box office. Had he made any attempt to rescue the people trapped inside, his clothes would not have remained as spotless as they were in the video. We realized that he had made no effort to save the patrons, but had instead focused on securing the day's collections to please his bosses.

There were also reports that claimed that legal luminaries had stated that a case should be registered against the owners of the cinema hall. In their opinion, the owners had invited people to visit their place without ensuring that the theatre was structurally safe to begin with. The media also reported that sources from the police force had said that there were specific orders from the ministry of home affairs to 'go slow' on some of the crucial aspects of the investigation, those that might stand against the owners.

Why had this happened only in the balcony? We kept asking ourselves this question over and over again, and finally decided to take legal recourse. Both of us did not know the workings of our country's criminal justice system. We had never been to any of the courts before this tragedy and hence, had no idea of their working.

Our first step was to find a lawyer who would fight our case with conviction. Over a dozen senior advocates were recommended. A friend, Shekhar Gupta, senior editor of a leading national daily, called us after the incident and advised us to seek a legal opinion from senior advocate K.T.S. Tulsi, who he said was a man of integrity and a public-spirited lawyer. He also told us that apart from following the criminal case, we should also file a civil case against the Ansals. He referred to the O.J. Simpson case, where the American football player was acquitted in the murder case, but was ordered to pay heavy compensatory and punitive damages in a civil case. Following his advice we contacted Tulsi on 27 June 1997. We were moved by his compassion when he offered to come home to see us, but we decided to meet him at his residence-cum-office in Sainik Farms.

The courts are closed for the summer in June, so we were surprised to see his entire team at his residence, including Sultan Singh, Vikas Pahwa and Hari Pillai. Tulsi was very sympathetic towards us and had strong views on those who seemed responsible for the tragedy. He told us that since the Ansals were part of the powerful builder lobby, we should fight this legal battle collectively. He suggested that we contact other affected families and form an association. When he told us that he would represent us pro bono, we were touched by his generosity and the hope of finding justice was kindled in our hearts.

We now had to contact the families of the other deceased, but we did not know any of them personally. We started by going through the obituary columns in the newspapers, in itself a herculean task. Not a single name seemed familiar and the only bond we shared with these strangers was that we had all lost our loved ones in the same fire. Steeling ourselves, we took the initiative and contacted members of the victims' families. Some were downright dismissive of our efforts, but a few of them listened to us very patiently.

Ultimately, nine families responded positively to us and we proposed a meeting.

The immediate family members of the victims were present at the first meeting, but they also brought along relatives, friends and well-wishers. At that first meeting, we were all a little uncomfortable with each other. Shekhar and I began a dialogue by speaking about our loss and grief. After listening to us, each of them opened up and shared their woes. We realized that we could share each other's sorrows and empathize with one another. Some had lost spouses and children, while others had lost their young sons or daughters. There was one instance where a whole family had been wiped out by the fire.

Over the course of the meeting, different opinions and suggestions emerged. While someone suggested that we protest publicly, others said that we should involve political parties. After listening to everybody's views, it was decided by a majority that the involvement of any political party should be ruled out. It was a well-known fact that some builder lobbies were politically connected and we were sceptical about receiving any support from their partners. Had we involved them, in all likelihood our fight for justice would have been sabotaged early in the day.

Shortly thereafter, we informed the families of the victims that we had approached K.T.S. Tulsi, who was of the opinion that the affected families should collectively pursue the fight to seek due punishment for the perpetrators of the crime. We also told them that he had agreed to fight our case pro bono.

Most of those present had little or no legal knowledge and wanted to understand the objective of us seeking justice through these channels. Following the popular belief about the lack of integrity of lawyers, some family members harboured doubts about Tulsi and voiced the fear that he might settle on a compromise with the Ansals. It took considerable persuasion from both of us to convince them that this would not happen. We related to them that he had been the additional solicitor general of India, had an impeccable character and was a man of integrity, whose name had been recommended to us by a very senior journalist. The families finally agreed to meet him on 30 June.

We all met at Tulsi's residence in Sainik Farms. He apprised the families of the legal remedies available to the victims, and made us understand the importance of fighting this battle collectively against the builder lobby and government agencies.

A Memorandum of Article and Association was prepared by nine founding members and we decided to call ourselves the Association of the Victims of Uphaar Tragedy. The association resolved to work together for a safe India and to save others from similar misfortune. We had the following objectives:

- To fight for justice and to take legal proceedings to their logical conclusion, so that there is deterrence and such man-made tragedies are not repeated.
- To create public awareness of criminal negligence on the part of public authorities and owners and occupiers of public places.
- To organize seminars, debates and workshops to highlight the lack of basic safety measures in public places.
- To ensure implementation of safety laws, rendered by all honourable courts in the country.
- To highlight the need for effective enforcement of safety rules and regulations.
- To examine legislation in the field of safety laws and to take measures to have the regulations upgraded, keeping in view the changing need of the times.

As various articles were filed by national dailies and magazines about the formation of AVUT, the other affected families, those we had been unable to reach, contacted us of their own volition and enrolled as members. AVUT was born of the anger and grief of the twenty-eight bereaved families. It was decided among us that only the first-degree heirs of the deceased would be permanent members of the association. It was also decided that though we would be fighting to get compensation for people who sustained injuries in the fire, they would not be enrolled as members of AVUT. This was to ensure that there was no infiltration or weakening of our stand.

After the meeting, some of the members felt the need to consult other lawyers and seek additional opinions, but ultimately they decided to proceed with Tulsi's advice.

There is a common perception among the media and courts that AVUT is an elite group of victims, but this is not so. They are probably unaware of the fact that we have members from different strata of society, and that it was grief and anger that brought us together. We were united by our mission to secure justice for our loved ones.

We decided to put together photographs of all the victims, with their names and ages written at the bottom. This was done to maintain the identity of the victims. At no stage did we want them to be known as the 'fifty-nine victims'; instead, we wanted them to be remembered by their names. The photographs were displayed on panels whenever we organized an event.

A common factor that angered all of us in AVUT was the insensitivity shown by the Ansals. The vice president (services) of the Ansal Group, one V.K. Nagpal, chose to blame those watching the film for the tragedy at Uphaar Cinema. According to him, the patrons had made a mistake by running out of the balcony. They should have just stayed put in the balcony and then they would have survived. 'We are not at fault,' he said. Their technical expert too maintained that had the people stayed inside the building they would have all survived. (*Indian Express*, 17 June 1997)

As if this were not bad enough, the Ansals went a step further and showed their arrogance and insensitivity by issuing a half-page advertisement in most leading national newspapers. The statements in the advertisement were intentionally misleading. The Uphaar management gave certain facts about the fire in an attempt to absolve itself of any responsibility. The management claimed that the fire had originated from a DVB transformer. They claimed that DVB had sanctioned electrical load for the theatre on the condition that they provide space for the transformer. The Delhi Fire Service had recommended its relocation, which was not heeded by DVB. The management had obtained clearances from various government agencies. The staff of the cinema and the management had saved and evacuated the patrons even at the risk of their own lives. There were sufficient fire extinguishers. The smoke travelled through the staircase and not through AC ducts. Finally, it said, Uphaar Cinema was owned by a company registered under the Company's Act. (*Times of India*, 23 June 1997)

The advertisement issued by the Uphaar management consisted of blatant lies. To us, it appeared as if the Ansals were adding insult to our grief. Instead of issuing a half-page wish of condolence or apology, and accepting responsibility for the loss of lives, they chose to use their wealth and power to spread falsehoods and absolve themselves of their wrongdoings. While one theatre owner published a condolence message in the newspapers, lamenting the untimely end of fifty-nine lives, we felt that the Ansals showed no signs of remorse.

Soon after the incident, in June itself, media reports too became increasingly more disturbing and we suspected that there was immense pressure on the investigating agency to soften their stand in order to safeguard the interests of the Ansals. On being questioned by the media about the status of the investigation on the liability of the Ansal brothers, we found that the police was very casual in their response and said that they are seeking the opinion of top lawyers with the evidence they had collected. The process of collection was still on and they said they have time on their side. If the Ansal brothers are liable in a criminal case, they would book them. It could well be that being real estate tycoons, they had strong political connections.

We were also deeply pained to read in the newspapers that the Army Wives Welfare Association, headed by the then army chief's wife, had scheduled the premiere of the film *Border* on the very day we were observing the thirteenth day rituals for the departed souls. The Uphaar incident had been widely reported across the nation and therefore, the association could not have been unaware of the implications of scheduling the premiere on a day when we were mourning an irreparable loss. How could they not have realized the special significance of the thirteenth day ceremony in our tradition or that scheduling the movie on that specific day would be disrespectful towards the dead and hurt the feelings of the grieving families? Even the remarks made by the then defence minister, who chose to be present at the said premiere, hurt our feelings. He is reported to have brushed aside a suggestion that the premiere was badly timed, merely remarking, 'You tend to attach sentiments to anything and everything.' (*Hindustan Times*, 25 June 1997)

7

Facts and Reports

On 3 July, Naresh Kumar, the deputy commissioner (south) filed his inquiry report, placing responsibility for lapses in security and evacuation measures on the cinema owners (the Ansals) and other government agencies— the Delhi Vidyut Board, deputy commissioner of police (Licensing), Delhi Fire Service (DFS) and the Municipal Corporation of Delhi (MCD).

We were enraged when we read the report, which included the responses of the Ansals to the questions posed by the inquiry committee. They claimed that the board of directors was not required to visit the premises nor was it required to do a risk management exercise, as its role was confined to taking major policy decisions. Further, the risk management exercise was not prescribed under any rule or directions from the authorities.

After reading the report, we assumed that what the Ansals had done in Uphaar was tantamount to wilful disobedience of rules with the sole purpose of increasing the number of seats in the balcony, closing the only exit available on the right-hand side and converting the same into a private box, and placing extra seats in the gangway with the clear intention of increasing profits, thus endangering human lives.

The blocked exit could have been a lifeline for the patrons on that fateful day. Instead, the balcony was converted into a gas chamber due to the thick, black, toxic smoke, coupled with the noxious fumes that rose from the ground floor where the DVB transformer was housed. The sudden power failure also caused the balcony to become pitch-dark. The absence of basic fire safety measures such as emergency lights, exit lights, a public address system, all of which are mandatory in a public space, only made it worse for the patrons, who could not find their way out in time and were trapped in the balcony.

The grossly inadequate number of exits, which were, to make matters worse, badly placed, aisles of inadequate width and the absence of visible signs over the exit doors, all added up to a veritable death trap for the viewers in the balcony. Furthermore, the exit on the lower left-hand side opened on to the staircase, which was full of fumes and smoke. So people had to find an alternative route to escape. This led to chaos and panic, and a number of people were trampled on in the ensuing confusion. The exit door at the upper level on the left side had been closed. This was admitted by Manmohan, a member of the staff on duty. Those patrons who managed to escape into the lobby found it engulfed in fumes and smoke. Gasping for breath, they rushed madly to the two toilets at the ends of the lobby. The lobby was air-conditioned, so there was no opening for fresh air and the desperate people tried to break the glass of the windows in a bid to escape.

The licensee was found totally unprepared for such an emergency. The staff on duty showed no sense of responsibility in the rescue work and, instead, ran for their lives. The assistant manager of the hall admitted that if the staff had been trained properly and if they had shown some sense of duty on that day, the casualties might have been far fewer. When the fire went out of control, the deputy general manager of the cinema ensured the cash was moved to a safer place and made sure his car was not in danger, instead of taking prompt action to save the patrons. The management abandoned the patrons to their fate and ran out of the cinema hall.

We were enraged to learn from the report that Uphaar Cinema was functioning based on a stay order granted by the Delhi High Court way back in 1983. This stay was granted, despite the safety regulations mentioned in the Cinematograph Rules being violated. This fact was pointed out by the licensing authority. The four-day stay granted by the High Court continued for fourteen long years, till the date of the incident, despite eleven deviations in the cinema hall pointed out by the authorities in 1983 and a serious fire in the cinema in 1989.

The Naresh Kumar report further revealed that as per the records of the licensing department, the cinema was never issued an annual license after April 1983. They were continuously issued temporary permits for durations of two months at a time since 1983 till the date of the tragedy.

After going through the inquiry report, we were not willing to accept the fire as something predestined. Tulsi told us that our first endeavour should be to file a petition under Article 32 in the Supreme Court, seeking punitive damages and uniform compensation for such a man-made disaster. Despite the tragedy having occurred within a kilometre of two premiere hospitals, they were not equipped to handle a catastrophe of this nature. Hence, the need for proper

trauma centres was also highlighted. This was one of the
main factors in our writ petition, wherein we sought Rs 100
crore as damages for the setting up of a much-needed trauma
centre. Ironically, this was not the first time the concept of
such a centre had been brought up. In fact, the need for this
had been felt way back in 1975 by the then health minister,
Dr Karan Singh, under the able advice of Dr Ramalinga
Swamy. In 1983, after a period of eight years, the proposed
project was shifted to the Delhi administration and 15 acres
of land was purchased adjacent to Safdarjung Hospital. The
foundation stone for the trauma centre was laid in 1991,
but nothing more was done in this direction.

After going through the facts as enumerated in the
report, we were confident that the case would be an open
and shut one, and we would have a verdict at the earliest.

On 13 September 1997, AVUT organized a panel
discussion titled 'How Safe are Cinema Halls in Delhi?'
We hosted some eminent speakers and each of them spoke
eloquently on the subject. One of the speakers was the
former lieutenant governor of Delhi, who questioned the
Delhi High Court's move to revoke the cancellation of
Uphaar's licence in 1983.

To recap, the licence of Uphaar Cinema had been
cancelled in 1983 by the Licensing Authority on account
of violation of fire safety norms. Despite various attempts
by the owners to revoke the cancellation, they did not get
any relief from the lieutenant governor. The Ansals then
approached the High Court and were successful in procuring
a stay for four days only, during which time they were meant
to rectify all violations. However, this stay continued till 13
June 1997, namely the day the tragedy occurred.

Another speaker, Tavleen Singh, a renowned journalist,
described the fire as a horror story and not just a tragedy.

When she recalled an incident which took place soon
after the Uphaar tragedy, an eerie silence descended in the
auditorium. She said that during her meeting with the then
lieutenant governor, the wife of the then finance secretary
called him up to inquire whether movie theatres in Delhi
were safe enough to send her children. He had said, 'No,
it isn't. Wait till it is safe.' What was startling was the
carelessness of his remarks.

After the discussion, we showed footage of the incident
procured from various news channels. Everyone in the
audience was in tears at the end of our video. People
could see how the smoke had engulfed the cinema hall and
billowed out of the windows. They saw footage of dead
bodies being carried out of the hall. Most AVUT members
were seeing this for the first time and some of them were
inconsolable when they spotted their loved ones among
the dead. As organizers of the discussion, it was impossible
for Shekhar and me to show any signs of breaking down,
but you can imagine how torturous it was for us to silently
watch footage of the tragedy.

Though October in 1997 was a month of festivals, there
were no celebrations for members of AVUT. We decided
that we would hold a prayer meeting outside Uphaar on
13 October, in the hope of securing some peace for our
loved ones. Although we had chosen the venue, we did not
anticipate the difficulties we would encounter while seeking
police permission. The police were reluctant to allow us to
hold a prayer meeting outside Uphaar Cinema and asked us
to look for an alternate site, but we were insistent. Senior
officers informed us that they feared conflict would break
out, because emotions were running very high and there
was a possibility that some members would get violent.
We assured them that the prayer meeting would be held

peacefully and there would be no untoward incident. With great reluctance, we were allowed to go ahead, but only with a large contingent of police personnel at the site. We decided to hold a prayer meet and requested Shubha Mudgal, a dear friend, to sing bhajans at the venue.

As she sang some heart-rending Kabir bhajans, most of those present at the meet could not control their emotions. A lot of passers-by and shopkeepers from the neighbouring areas too joined us. The atmosphere was sombre and moving, not just for the families of the victims but for all those who had joined in. We were touched when several members of the public gave floral tributes to the departed souls. Some shopkeepers even came up to us and informed us of what had happened on that fateful day, and how each one of them had done their bit to save lives. Some of them had harrowing tales to tell. Tears rolled down our faces when we heard that the shopkeepers had provided mattresses to enable trapped patrons to jump from the upper floors of the building. They also told us that since there were no ambulances, they had helped carry the victims in their own cars and vehicles. There had been no help from the cinema staff, since all of them had fled to save their own skins.

It was on this day that we identified a small park outside Uphaar Cinema, where we wanted to build and maintain a small memorial to the victims. The park was in a dilapidated condition and was used as a dump yard by the local shopkeepers. We were told that the park belonged to the MCD and was leased to Uphaar Cinema for maintenance.

AVUT approached MCD and, in 1998, a Memorandum of Understanding was signed where they let us maintain the park. The memorial, made using black granite, that stands here now is engraved with the names and the date of birth of each of the fifty-nine deceased, embossed like the dials of a watch, frozen in time by an event whose ripples have travelled far and wide. '. . . Until justice rolls down like water and righteousness like a mighty stream . . .' These lines by Martin Luthur King Jr are inscribed on the wall. They sum up the feelings and expectations of the affected families. A stream of water flows continuously on the round structure in front of the wall that bears the names of all the victims. This stream is supposed to serve as a constant reminder of the pain and trauma that the victims' families are going through, and the hope for justice we sustain amid the darkness of despair. The memorial is called 'Smriti Upavan'.

Public memory being short, the Uphaar tragedy would have been on the back-burner had it not been for AVUT's endeavours to keep its memory alive. We organized panel discussions, seminars, blood donation camps and inter-school debates on the thirteenth of each month to coincide with the date of the incident. We took up issues relating to food safety, road safety, corruption, and the role of private and government hospitals in emergency care.

We were incensed that even a year after the tragedy, Sushil Ansal, the owner of the cinema, showed no signs of remorse and in an interview with a leading national daily, shrugged off all responsibility for the tragedy. He insisted that they were in no way responsible for the incident. In fact, he compared the tragedy to a road accident involving a truck, and said that when an accident takes place, the truck is returned to the owner in a day or two. It is not held by the investigating agency for years on end. An accident had taken place, but this did not mean that the building should not be returned to the owners, he tried to reason. Shockingly, he added that he was not repentant about the Uphaar tragedy, though he now claims to have been sad about the whole affair. We thought this was a very callous remark. To compare and equate the tragic loss of innocent lives with road accidents and matters pertaining to property disputes can only be an indication of the insensitivity of those who make such statements. Did he not pause to think, for even a second, that our children would never return to us, whether or not his trucks and properties were returned to him?

Thus began a long legal battle. Our journey to get justice was full of obstacles, hindrances, uncertainties and what felt like a never-ending struggle. But what kept us going was our patience, perseverance, courage, conviction and determination, and the memories of the happy times we spent with our children.

It was not an easy task to take up a legal battle for which we were neither trained nor experienced. We were novices and had plunged into these shark-infested waters because our children, as well as the fifty-seven other people, were not destined to die. They were all murdered. To us it seems as if it was an incident of mass murder, since all the rules had been violated. Fifty-nine innocent people had to pay with their lives only because of this.

In the process of coping with immense personal loss and tragedy, and in the face of the unimaginable frustration that the legal process in India forces on litigants, there were occasions when some of our members lost their will to persevere. Fortunately, with a little counselling from Shekhar and me, the association stayed together and has stood the ultimate test of time.

8

The Investigation

The initial investigation into the Uphaar Cinema fire was handled by the Hauz Khas police station. The first information report (FIR) was lodged on the basis of a complaint made by the security guard of the hall. The Delhi Police lodged the FIR under section 304 (II), i.e. culpable homicide not amounting to murder with a punishment of up to ten years in prison. Considering the gravity of the incident, the investigation was then transferred to the Crime Branch of the Delhi Police.

As per media reports, the police arrested the four managers of the cinema and a senior electrical fitter of the electricity board. We were appalled that the police were showing hesitation to even examine the culpability of the Ansals, and repeatedly claimed there wasn't enough evidence to prosecute the well-known builders. It was reported in the papers: 'Faced with the criticism of "selective action", senior police officers on the condition of anonymity have said that they were under "extreme pressure" from the Union home ministry not to touch the Ansals.' (*Hindustan Times*, 22 June 1997)

The then commissioner of police, in an interview to the press, stated that the directors and managers were directly responsible for running the cinema. The involvement of the Ansals was being investigated and action would be taken only after the investigation was completed. He added that they would follow the course of law and could not take any action against them at this stage. (*Pioneer*, 18 June 1997)

Initially, confusion regarding ownership of the cinema persisted. Finally, on 8 July 1997, the Delhi Police managed to interrogate the owner, Sushil Ansal. He was questioned for over four hours with regard to the ownership of Uphaar Cinema, and his movements on and after 13 June. Ansal claimed that he had left for Bangalore on 13 June at around 4 p.m. On being asked why he did not join the investigation, he is believed to have said that he had panicked and was afraid. The police asked him to be present for further questioning on 9 July.

When Sushil Ansal did not appear for further questioning on the designated date, the Delhi Police launched a search and carried out several raids in his office and his residence. They even tried to interrogate his brother, Gopal Ansal, who was reported to be in London.

On 17 July, members of AVUT met the lieutenant governor of Delhi, and requested him to expedite the investigation and not to delay the filing of the charge sheet. During the meeting, we also told him that the police seemed rather soft on the Ansals. The members also submitted a memorandum demanding the registration of an FIR against the owners of the cinema hall for tampering with evidence in collusion with officials of various government departments, including the Licensing Authority and Registrar of Companies. The lieutenant governor told us that it had come to his notice and an FIR had been lodged to this effect. To our shock and disappointment, he gave us no assurance regarding a possible arrest of the Ansals. Since we demanded speedy action against the guilty, he pleaded for time until 10 August, but did not give us any reason for asking for this extra time. Surprisingly, he claimed to be unaware of the non-availability of oxygen masks in the ambulance or with the firemen, and the lack of facilities at AIIMS to deal with asphyxia. He was also not aware of the fact that of the six ambulances in AIIMS, only one had been operational on 13 June.

As we discovered the lethargy of the administrative system, several rumours were also brought to our notice about the connections the Ansals enjoyed with people in power, which eventually may have resulted in intentional delays by the investigating agency in arresting the Ansal brothers. However, we had no way of investigating these rumours, although we still question that month when there was no sign of the Ansals (but for a single appearance by Sushil Ansal on 8 July), who seemed to have vanished into thin air. It would have been impossible for any ordinary citizen to have disappeared like this, unless they have close connections with the people in power. Nineteen years down the line, such rumours and whispers do not seem so incredible to us when we witness powerful and wealthy people disappearing when the first sign of trouble appears.

Our grievance was that the culprits who caused the tragedy were still at large, more than a month after the incident. We wanted to highlight this glaring lapse to the prime minister, and inform him of the inaction on the part of the lieutenant governor and the home secretary. We wanted to share with him our scepticism regarding the government's intentions. Though the Naresh Kumar report had identified those responsible for the mishap in a mere eighteen days, the government was dithering and not taking action against the accused.

The members of the association made a sincere effort to get an audience with the prime minister, just for fifteen minutes, in order to apprise him of the situation and receive the assurance that the perpetrators of one of the worst man-made disasters in recent times would be brought to justice. But we found ourselves facing the impenetrable wall of bureaucracy. Our fax requests went unanswered and officials in the Prime Minister's Office (PMO) remained unsympathetic to our request, as so many others had been. Around the same time, the then prime minister took time out from his busy schedule to meet a girl from the UK, who was in India leading a campaign to save tigers, but he had no time for the families of the fifty-nine victims.

It was appalling that the prime minister of the country could not spare fifteen minutes, roughly fifteen seconds per dead person, from his busy schedule to meet the families of the victims. In stark contrast to this, the prime minister of South Korea resigned on moral grounds after the ferry accident in April 2014, which claimed the lives of over 400 children. After the recent fire in a nightclub in Bucharest, Romania, in October 2015, where thirty-two people died, the prime minister and his entire cabinet resigned, accepting moral responsibility for the incident. Are we wrong to assume that the lives of ordinary citizens are of much greater value in Romania and South Korea than in India?

Thanks to constant pressure from AVUT, the Crime Branch finally approached the magistrate's court for permission to arrest Sushil and Gopal Ansal, and issue non-bailable warrants. During the course of the investigation, the Crime Branch also incorporated sections 468 (forgery for purpose of cheating), 471 (using as genuine a forged document), 201 (tampering with evidence), with section 120 B (conspiracy) of the Indian Penal Code (IPC). Since Gopal Ansal was not joining the investigation, an intimation was also sent to Interpol for a lookout notice against him.

Sushil Ansal and his son, Pranav, were arrested by the Delhi Police in Mumbai on 22 July 1997. We were quite hopeful that the charge sheet would be filed soon and the investigation into the case expedited. But, to our utter shock and disbelief, the Government of India took a suo moto decision to transfer the case to the Central Bureau of Investigation (CBI) on 23 July. It was our belief that this was done with the motive of delaying the filing of the charge sheet and, in the process, making it possible for the accused to seek and obtain bail. There was a sudden change in the approach of the counsel for the CBI in the High Court on 25 July 1997, with regard to the bail of the four managers of Uphaar Cinema. It took us by complete surprise that while the Delhi Police had been consistently opposing the granting of bail for two weeks, the CBI, in the very first hearing, agreed to grant them bail, even before it had taken charge of the case diaries from the Delhi Police. Today, as we watch TV debates about the possibility of politicians influencing the integrity of agencies like the CBI, which has even been referred to as 'caged parrots' by the Supreme Court, our fears in this regard can no longer be called unjustified or brushed under the carpet.

All the accused who were arrested were granted bail. After barely spending a month in jail, Sushil and Pranav Ansal were also granted bail on 22 August 1997.

Gopal Ansal was never arrested. He got anticipatory bail on 3 September 1997 by the High Court, while he was still in the United Kingdom. Intimation was sent to Interpol for deleting his name from the National Computer Network of wanted persons and to immigration authorities to allow him to proceed to India.

Once the case was transferred to the CBI, we were certain that the investigation would have to begin from scratch again and the process would get further delayed. This move by the government frustrated the victims' families and the survivors. We, along with other members of the association, once again made efforts to meet the prime minister and the home minister, but the PMO and the home ministry were very dismissive.

As we suspected, the CBI took time investigating the matter and failed to file the charge sheet within the stipulated period of sixty days from the date of the offence. As a result, all the accused were granted bail.

The CBI finally filed the charge sheet on 15 November 1997, indicting sixteen accused, including Sushil and Gopal Ansal. The CBI looked into the chain of events that led to the incident and their investigation revealed that there had been a fire in the DVB transformer at 6.55 a.m. on 13 June. The transformer was repaired and electricity was restored at 11.30 a.m. The improper repair of the transformer by the DVB employees that morning had led to the second fire in the evening and the entry of smoke into the auditorium and balcony.

The report also examined the cause behind the DVB transformer malfunctioning. The agency looked into the fire safety norms and the deviations in the Uphaar Cinema building to determine whether these digressions had contributed to the fire and hindered the escape of those seated in the balcony. It collected a fire report from the DFS with regard to the rescue operations conducted by the personnel on 13 June, which clearly stated that about 160 people had been rescued—among them 100 persons were conscious and about sixty unconscious. Of these, fifty-seven were declared dead in the hospital. The report further stated that most of the casualties were recovered from the balcony, toilets, the lobby outside the balcony and the adjoining offices.

Since no post-mortem of the victims was done at AIIMS and Safdarjung Hospital, the only one conducted was by the Army Hospital on one of the victims, which revealed that cause of death was asphyxiation due to inhalation of a combination of toxic gases, including carbon monoxide.

During the course of the investigation, the CBI seized several documents relating to Uphaar Cinema from the Delhi Fire Service, Municipal Corporation of Delhi, Public Works Department, the deputy commissioner of police (licensing) Delhi Police, Delhi Vidyut Board and the office of Ansal Theatre & Clubotels Pvt. Ltd. It also involved various agencies like the Central Forensic Science Laboratory (CFSL), Central Building Research Institute (CBRI), forensic science experts from the AIIMS medical board, technical experts from PWD, MCD and the electrical inspector from the national capital territory of Delhi. Statements from a large number of witnesses, the causes and effects of the incident, were also recorded.

In September 1976, the lieutenant governor issued a notification permitting cinema halls in Delhi to add certain seats to offset the losses caused due to the government's move to deduct rates by 10 per cent during the Emergency. As a result of this notification, forty-three seats were added in the balcony and fifty-seven seats in the main hall of Uphaar Cinema. In July 1979, the lieutenant governor issued another notification cancelling the 1976 notification. This was challenged by several cinema hall owners, including the owners of Uphaar Cinema, in the High Court. In its judgment in November 1979, the High Court upheld the right of the lieutenant governor to withdraw the relaxation. It also directed the Licensing Authority to determine which cinema halls had contravened which rule and to what extent. Allow only those seats which are in substantial compliance of the rules, the High Court told the Licensing Authority.

Pursuant to the order, the then DCP (Licensing Authority) personally inspected Uphaar Cinema and allowed thirty-seven out of the forty-three seats to be retained in the balcony, even though they blocked the right-hand side gangway. He also completely overlooked the additional private box built by the Ansals which blocked the exit on the right side. However, he ordered that the fifty-six additional seats be removed from the auditorium as these seats blocked the vertical gangways leading to the exit.

The investigation further revealed that Gopal Ansal had, in 1978, sought permission from authorities for an additional eight-seater box for personal use. We were shocked to read the contents of the letter wherein Gopal Ansal had thanked the   authorities for sanctioning a fourteen-seater private box for the family. He requested another eight-seater box, stating that the family was growing and hence, they should be sanctioned an additional private box. By blocking the exit that could have led many innocent people to safety on that fateful day, the Ansals showed no concern for the families and the precious lives of innocent victims—instead, they chose to provide comforts and luxury for their own family members. While their family grew, ours and those of many others were brutally cut short.

In 1980, Gopal Ansal sought permission for another fifteen seats; these were to be installed in the balcony on the left-hand side. Out of these nine seats, which reduced the width of the gangway, six seats were placed right in front of the exit on the upper tier, which obstructed the rapid dispersal of the patrons.

In its report, CFSL highlighted that the fire had originated in the DVB transformer. It also explained how the smoke had travelled up the stairwell, due to a chimney effect. It further detailed the spread of smoke into the hall and the balcony. As per its report, ten of the twenty-two fire extinguishers had been empty and five others were not in working order.

The CBRI in its report stated that the spillage of transformer oil resulted in the fire reaching a car that was parked outside the transformer room, which led to the subsequent gutting of all the cars in the vicinity. It also explained how the smoke travelled from the ground floor to the balcony through a small opening with a diameter of about 45 cm in the roof of the ground floor. It was this that was responsible for the spread of the smoke into the hall through AC ducts.

The department of Forensic Medicine and Toxicology, AIIMS, stated that forty-one patients had been brought dead to AIIMS. On the basis of the post-mortem report from the Army Hospital and the CFSL report, the board was of the opinion that the deaths had all occurred due to carbon monoxide poisoning. The board had come to the conclusion that there were no burn injuries or any evidence of a stampede. It further opined that the combined effect of various toxic gases produced during combustion might have caused the rapid death of the victims.

Sixteen patients were declared brought dead to Safdarjung Hospital. Two patients subsequently died during the course of treatment at AIIMS.

The technical experts from MCD and PWD gave floor-wise details of the violations and deviations done by the Uphaar management that contrasted with the original sanctioned plan approved by the MCD.

Sushil and Gopal Ansal were charge sheeted under sections 304 A (cause of death by negligence), 337 (causing hurt by endangering life or personal safety of others), 338 (causing grievous hurt by act of endangering life or personal safety of others) and read with section 36 (effect caused partly by act and partly by omission) of the IPC for their negligent acts of omission and commission—of allowing the installation of the DVB transformer, various structural and fire safety deviations in the building in violation of rules and not facilitating the escape of patrons, thus causing the death of fifty-nine persons and injuries to 100 others. The charge sheet further revealed that the Ansals had complete financial control of the cinema. As per the records of the Registrar of Companies, the entire shareholding of the company was held by the Ansal family, consisting of a total of 5000 equity shares.

R.M. Puri (director of the cinema and the brother-in-law of Sushil and Gopal Ansal), four managers of Uphaar Cinema and the gatekeeper were charge sheeted with commission of offences punishable under sections 304 (punishment for culpable homicide not amounting to murder), 337 and 338 and read with section 36 of the IPC.

Three employees of DVB were charged sheeted under sections 304, 337, 338 and read with section 36 of the IPC. Two employees of MCD, two employees of DFS and one employee from the Public Works Department (PWD) were charge sheeted under sections 304 A, 337, 338 and read with section 36 of the IPC.

As per the documents seized by the CBI, prima facie (a fact presumed to be true unless it is disproved) there was enough evidence to show that if the management had ensured proper safety precautions were in place and had not increased the number of seats in the balcony, if they had not blocked the gangway on the right side in order to install additional seats and closed the right exit to create a private viewing box for the Ansal family, all the patrons could have been saved. It was evident from the charge sheet that the owners and occupiers had held scant regard for the safety of the patrons. There were a number of structural and other fire safety deviations, including the absence of any means of escape, no trained firemen on site, no fire alarm system, no emergency lights and no public address system. Every rule of the statute had been violated. These deviations were committed with the knowledge of Sushil and Gopal Ansal, who continued to control the management and affairs of the hall, even on the day of the incident.

The executive engineer of the PWD was charge sheeted for closure of the exit and allowing extra seats in the balcony, contrary to established rules. The officers of the MCD were charge sheeted for unauthorized issue of a no objection certificate, which had been done without inspecting the hall from the structural point of view. The officers from DFS were charge sheeted for issuing a no objection certificate without carrying out inspections. As per official records, the charged officer was on casual leave the day he was supposed to have inspected the hall.

The officers of the DVB were charge sheeted for improper repair of the transformer on the morning of 13 June. Every rule in the book had been contravened, putting the lives of the patrons in danger.

The reason given by the home ministry for transferring the case to the CBI was that the Licensing Authority of the Delhi Police had been responsible for the issue of Uphaar Cinema's cinematograph licence. Hence, if the Delhi Police conducted the investigation, it would be prejudiced. However, none of the officers of the Delhi Police (Licensing Authority) were charge sheeted. It was evident from the documents that the then DCP (licensing) had allowed retention of additional seats, which blocked the gangway, and completely overlooked the closure of the right side exit when he inspected the cinema hall. This was the major reason why the patrons had been trapped in the balcony. The CBI did not charge sheet the officer presumably because at some point he had served as a senior official in the department. It merely recommended a departmental inquiry against him.

The CBI seemed under so much pressure that they invoked section 304 A of the IPC (rash and negligent acts) against Sushil and Gopal Ansal, contrary to the section 304 (II) (culpable homicide not amounting to murder) invoked by the Delhi Police in their FIR. Despite the fact that there was ample evidence for the CBI to charge sheet the owners under section 304 (II) IPC, it chose to charge under a lighter section. The CBI did not charge the Ansals under sections 468, 471 and 201, read with section 120 B, which were for graver offences incorporated by the Crime Branch of the Delhi Police. Section 468 of the IPC is punishable with imprisonment for a term of seven years.

It is a well-known fact that the CBI comes directly under the PMO. Since the government had taken a suo moto decision to transfer the case to the CBI, we felt that this had been done with an ulterior motive. The charge sheet was intentionally diluted by invoking a lighter section of the penal code. Since this now became a bailable offence, the culprits would never be incarcerated until the matter was adjudicated by the Supreme Court decades later.

The CBI, during its investigation, did not take into consideration the 1989 fire that had broken out in the hall. In that case both the DVB as well as the cinema transformers caught fire, and the toxic gases and thick black smoke entered the hall. This alone could have been grounds for the CBI to invoke section 304 (II) of the IPC against Sushil and Gopal Ansal, as this implies knowledge of a potential mishap, which is a key requirement to be charged under this section.

The CBI should have thoroughly investigated the 1989 fire incident and called the then chief fire officer to record his statement. In an interview with a leading daily on 16 June 1997, the officer had said that in 1989, a similar fire had taken place in the transformer; it spread in the same manner and he had fought that fire. It had started in the transformer, had reached the parked vehicles, but before it could travel up to the hall, the movie watchers got to know of the fire. One thing he remembered distinctly from that incident was that when the people ran out of the hall in panic, they left their footwear behind. After the firefighting operation was over, the shoes and slippers lying inside the hall were picked up and put in large gunny bags. There must have been five or six bags of shoes collected from that incident.

Another fire official said that the cinema hall staff stationed in the vicinity noticed the fire and fled the site. Hundreds of avid movie watchers sat glued to their seats. The night show of the latest blockbuster went on. However, the fire department received a call about a crackle originating from the transformer. The caller, a cinema hall staffer, said there was dense smoke billowing around. The fire service personnel found on arrival that the fire had already engulfed the vehicles that were in the parking lot. The fire had been serious even then. (*Times of India*, 16 June 1997)

This evidence was enough to charge the owner/occupier of the hall under 304 (II) IPC since they had knowledge that there was a potential threat to the lives of cinemagoers. It's ironic that the CBI chose to invoke section 304 (II) of the IPC against the director, managers and gatekeeper who were working under the directions of the Ansal brothers, but charge sheeted the owners themselves under a lighter section. As per the correspondence seized from various departments, it was the Ansal brothers who sought permission for additional seats in the balcony, which blocked the gangway, and the installation of an eight-seater family box, which closed the only exit on the right-hand side of the balcony. The permission sought and granted was in total contravention of the Delhi Cinematograph Rules (DCR) and the Delhi Fire Prevention and Fire Safety Rules 1987. Some of the important rules contravened by the owners are enumerated below:

1. DCR 1953 First Schedule
Rule 15(2)
Parking arrangements: 'No vehicle shall be parked or allowed to stand in such a way as to obstruct exits or impede the rapid disposal of the persons accommodated in the event of fire or panic.'

Rule 7
Seating: The seating in the building shall be so arranged so that there is free access to exits.

Rule 8
Gangway:
Rule 8(1): Gangways not less than 44" wide shall be provided in the building as follows:
(a) Down each side of the auditorium;
(b) Down the centre of the seating accommodation at intervals of not more than 25 feet;
(c) Parallel to the line of the seating so as to provide direct access to an exit, provided that not more than one gangway for every ten rows shall be required.

Rule 8(4): The exits and gangways and passages leading to exits shall be kept clear of obstructions.

Rule 9(1)
Stairways: There shall be at least two stairways of width not less than 4 feet wide to provide access to any gallery or upper floor in the building which is intended for use by the public.

Rule 10
Rule 10(2): Exits: In the auditorium there shall be at least one exit from every tier, floor or gallery for every 100 persons.
Rule 10(4): Exit from the auditorium to be suitably placed along both sides and along back thereof and shall deliver into two or more different thoroughfares or open spaces from which there is at all times free means of rapid dispersal.
Rule 10(8): All exit doors and doors through which the public have to pass on the way to the open air shall be available for exit during the whole time that the public are in the building and during such time shall not be locked or bolted.

Rule 16(4)
Fire Precautions: During an exhibition all fire extinguishing appliances shall be in charge of some person or persons specially appointed for this purpose. Such persons need not be employed exclusively in looking after the fire appliances but they must not be given any other work during an exhibition which would take them away from the building or otherwise prevent them from being immediately available in case of danger or alarm of fire.

2. DCR 1981 First Schedule
Rule 19 (9 IV)
A report of any fire or alarm of fire, however slight shall be at once sent to the fire brigade.

3. Delhi Fire Prevention and Safety Rules 1987
Rule 5
Minimum standards: The minimum standards for fire prevention and fire safety measures specified for buildings or premises shall be as are provided in building by-laws notified in 1983 or as may be amended from time to time thereafter relating to following matters:

1. Means of access
2. Underground/overhead water static tanks
3. Automatic sprinkler system
4. First aid hose reels
5. Fire extinguisher of ISI certification mark
6. Compartmentation
7. Automatic fire detection and alarm system/manually operated fire alarm system
8. Public address system
9. Illuminated exit way marking signs
10. Alternate source of electric supply
11. Fire lift with fireman switch
12. Wet-Riser and Downcomer Systems

9

In India, Lives Come Cheap

There were two cases filed against the Ansals—one criminal and the other civil. The criminal case was filed by the CBI, which was the prosecuting agency. AVUT filed a civil writ petition under Article 32 of the Constitution of India in the Supreme Court against the owners and various government agencies for their lapses to pay compensation.

There can be no possible compensation for the loss of precious lives. AVUT sought, as a deterrent to future wrongdoers, compensation for the victims and punitive damages against the respondents for showing callous disregard of their statutory obligations, and the fundamental and indefeasible rights guaranteed under Article 21 of the Constitution. The startling revelations in the Naresh Kumar inquiry report were ample ground for AVUT to approach the Supreme Court under Article 32, which deals with remedies for the enforcement of fundamental rights. The Supreme Court directed that the writ be filed in the Delhi High Court under Article 226 of the Constitution, since the matter was related to the NCT. Article 226 deals with the power of the

High Courts to issue certain writs and can be invoked not only for the enforcement of fundamental rights, but for any other purpose as well.

Subsequently, a writ was filed in the High Court making the Union of India, M/s Ansal Theatre and Clubotels (P) Ltd (earlier known as Green Park Theatre Associated (P) Ltd), the owners, Sushil Ansal and Gopal Ansal, directors of the company, cinema management, DCP (licensing) the Delhi Police, Municipal Corporation of Delhi, Delhi Vidyut Board, ministry of health as respondents. In all, there were about forty respondents for the writ filed in the High Court, as AVUT wanted any individual or organization that could have contributed directly or indirectly to the Uphaar tragedy to be held responsible. The main aspects of the petition were:

- to ensure that no cinema hall in the country is allowed to run without a valid licence
- award damages to the tune of Rs 20 crore for the deceased and injured
- the respondents to pay a sum of Rs 100 crore for the augmentation of centralized accident and trauma services and other allied services in the city of Delhi

We included the trauma centre in our writ petition because the AIIMS and the Safdarjung Hospital were totally unprepared to handle such a disaster. There were very few ambulances to transport the injured/unconscious persons from the theatre, which was located just a kilometre away. Most of the injured and unconscious persons were taken to the hospital in PCR vans. Some were also taken by private vehicles, some by SDM's vehicles and some others by local tempos. The hospitals were also not informed at the outset about the casualties. The local police sent the station house officer, Defence Colony, to AIIMS to inform the doctors about the sheer scale of the tragedy, but only after the situation at the site took a turn for the worse. Safdarjung Hospital did not receive any message, according to the doctors. The staff on duty at the mortuary there and the outpatient department in AIIMS, where the dead bodies were kept, was very uncooperative.

While our writ petition was being heard on 26 October 1998, the additional solicitor general, appearing for the Union of India, pointed out to the judge that the latter could not adjudicate the matter, since he had appeared as a standing counsel for the NCT in a case involving Uphaar Cinema in a civil writ petition in 1983. The judge had to recuse himself from the matter and it was referred back to the chief justice of the Delhi High Court. This was the first legal hurdle we had to face. But it did not stop here.

The matter was listed before another judge on 30 October 1998. After that, further hearing was scheduled on 10 December. When we reached the court to attend the proceedings on the designated day, we were informed that the judge had been elevated to the Supreme Court and the matter would now be referred back to the chief justice to constitute a new bench. It was posted in front of another division bench and came up for hearing after seven weeks, i.e. on 29 January 1999. The matter was posted to be heard on 12 April 1999 and was to be taken up on a day-to-day basis.

Then due to the demise of the chief justice of the Delhi High Court, one of the judges listening to our case took over as the acting chief justice. Consequently, the matter was listed before another division bench. As luck would have it, one of the judges recused himself from the case and our hope for day-to-day hearings was shattered. The matter was referred back to the chief justice and was listed again on 6 May 1999. At this stage, the maintainability of our writ petition was challenged by the respondents on the grounds that it involved disputed facts and it was not appropriate for deciding the causation and responsibility for the unfortunate incident. On 13 July 1999, the counsel for the Ansals pointed out during the hearing that one of the judges had been a state counsel and had appeared in some related matters. Hence, the judge had to recuse himself. By now, we had understood that the Ansals and their lawyers were looking for opportunities to delay the case.

On 19 July 1999, the matter was taken up for hearing by the chief justice himself. Although the counsel for the Ansals made another attempt to stall by pointing out to the chief justice that his co-judge had been a standing counsel and had appeared in a matter relating to Uphaar Cinema in 1979, the bench refused to consider it as the matter had been adjudicated and would have no bearing on the ongoing case.

The bench heard the case on maintainability, which in layman's terms refers to whether the petition is filed before the proper forum and if the court has the jurisdiction to entertain the case. The case dragged on for over two months, but by this time more than two years had passed since the tragedy. Any hope that Shekhar and I had harboured of getting swift and speedy justice for our children dimmed steadily as loopholes in the legal system gave way to hurdles at every step.

The talk among those who walked the corridors of the justice system was that nothing would come of the case. On numerous occasions, we heard the advocates for the Ansals talk among themselves, saying that the very maintainability of our writ would be dismissed. One afternoon, after the hearing, when we were walking down the stairs of the High Court, we overheard a senior counsel for a government agency telling his clients that such accidents kept occurring and courts would never award such a whopping sum as compensation to the victims. He said that our case was nothing but media hype, which would die down with time.

In another incident, a counsel for another government respondent said that associations are made, but they can never withstand a prolonged legal battle. In fact, one of these counsels walked up to us and advised us to file a civil suit since the court would never award such a high compensation under Article 226. As might be expected, these statements disheartened us greatly.

In October 1999, arguments were being advanced by the counsel for the Ansals, saying that the cause of the tragedy was the fire in the DVB transformer and not the non-availability of exits, the blocked gangway, the non-functioning PA system, emergency lights and exit lights in the balcony. This counsel stated that people could have used cigarette lighters to find a way out or they could have jumped over the wall of the eight-seater box to exit the balcony. They must have known only too well that one of the gases produced by the burning transformer oil, car seats, foam and wood was cyanogen gas, which is highly flammable. This was confirmed by the report of the CFSL. So their suggestion of using lighters was ridiculous. Had lighters been used, the whole hall would have blown up, resulting in far more casualties.

At exactly this moment, the power supply in the court premises was disrupted, plunging the courtroom into darkness. Our counsel drew the court's attention to what might have transpired on the fateful evening of 13 June. The chief justice responded by wondering whether the defence counsels could try to find their way out of the courtroom in the darkness. They had no answer to that. (*Indian Express*, 2 October 1999)

The counsels for the defence suggested that these cases be decided out of court, failing which it would open the floodgates for future tragedies. The judges responded that it was up to the parties involved to decide on this.

29 February 2000. More than two and a half years after the tragedy, our judgment on the maintainability of the writ was to be delivered. The High Court lawyers were on strike. Tulsi's chamber received a call from the High Court, informing him that because of the lawyers' strike the judgment could not be pronounced in the open court. We were informed by his office to be present in the court at 2 p.m. that afternoon. It was an anxious moment for us, since this was the first judgment to be delivered. Despite negative feedback from the lawyers, we were very optimistic of the judgment being in our favour. We asked the other members of AVUT to be present in court as well.

The members reached the court at 1.30 p.m. We found the courtroom packed with media personnel and advocates from other parties. The lawyers were called into the judge's chamber at 2 p.m. All other parties were asked to wait in the courtroom. We silently prayed and hoped for a favourable judgment because this would, in a sense, decide our course of action in the future.

An hour passed without any news and the tension kept mounting. In hushed tones, the members of the association kept asking us why it was taking so much time. Finally, we saw Tulsi walking out of the judge's chamber into the courtroom, his smile an indication of AVUT's first victory. He informed us that the writ had been maintained against the Union of India, Ansal Theatre and Clubotels (P) Ltd, the ministry of health, DCP (licensing), Delhi Police, Municipal Corporation of Delhi, Delhi Vidyut Board and other government agencies. He also told us that the judge had constituted a commission of three members to look into the deviations and violations in the cinema hall, for which a fee of Rs 1 lakh had to be paid.

Since the Union of India, Ansal Theatre and Clubotels and the other government agencies were not willing to bear the cost, AVUT had no option but to agree to bear the fees. As the case proceeded, we had our first taste of the legal system and its many injustices. To begin with, we realized with shock and distress that while multimillionaires like the Ansals refused to pay the fee of Rs 1 lakh, victims like us were expected to cough up the amount or else lose the battle before it even began. Anyone who approaches the court seeking justice should be prepared for setbacks and shocks such as these. Has no luminary ever pondered on the many injustices embedded so deeply in the legal system, which permit grieving victims to be pushed against the wall even in the face of immense personal tragedy?

We could not comprehend why the Union of India, which is honour-bound as per Article 21 of the Constitution to protect its people, refused to pay the fee. We finally reached the conclusion that the strategy adopted by the Ansals and the government agencies was to ensure that the case hit roadblock after roadblock to dissuade us from pursuing it. Thanks to being an association, we were in a position to collect and raise the funds to pay the fees, but had the court been just, it would have directed all the respondents to bear the costs collectively.

The court held that as per the provisions of law, where questions of life and liberty arise, it would not be justified to require that the party seeking relief go through the lengthy and expensive process of a civil suit. A party claiming to be aggrieved by the action of a public body or authority is entitled to a hearing of its petition. Despite the declared intention of providing swift justice, loopholes in the legal system permitted an enormous delay in our case.

But it cannot be denied that the maintainability of the writ under Article 226 of the constitution was a landmark judgment. A major hurdle had been crossed.

10

A Heart-breaking Visit

The court commissioners had to visit Uphaar Cinema and submit a report about whether or not all the rules, regulations and statutory provisions had been complied with and if not, to what extent they had been violated. They were also meant to ascertain whether there had been any unauthorized deviations from these rules. It was decided that representatives of all the parties could accompany the commissioners during their visit. We decided to go too since we were privy to the reports of the technical experts on the state of the site. We also sought help from an architect, asking him to study the building plan to understand the layout of the cinema hall before accompanying the commissioners on their visit. This meant that we were, in fact, mapping the very location where our lovely children had breathed their last.

As the day for the inspection loomed, we were very apprehensive about visiting Uphaar Cinema. We struggled to assess whether we would be able to withstand more emotional and psychological trauma. Unable to sleep the night before the inspection, we tossed and turned in bed, but finally decided to go ahead in the morning. We knew that if we decided to nurse our grief, we would forever lose the opportunity to prove beyond doubt that the many violations and deviations were responsible for the death of our children. It was of the utmost importance for us to know that the inspection had been conducted meticulously, without adopting any shortcuts.

To enter the cinema hall was, in a sense, to relive the trauma and loss we had suffered. When we reached Uphaar Cinema, we found media personnel, staff of the Ansals, representatives from various government agencies and the lawyers were all present. We were waiting for the commissioners to arrive. This was the first time after the incident that Uphaar would be opened up to the victims' families and other parties. There were several onlookers present outside the hall, curious to know the purpose of the visit. Some local shopkeepers were hopeful that after this visit, the hall would reopen. Once they learnt the purpose of our visit, they were disappointed and some even became extremely hostile towards us. We understood that the closure of the cinema hall meant a loss of business for them and we do not hold any grudge against them for their behaviour.

Once the commissioners arrived, CBI officials unlocked the side door on the ground floor allowing us to enter the hall. Before entering the hall, the representatives of all the parties involved in the case had to sign a register maintained by the CBI. As everyone else entered the hall, I was hesitant as I could not control my emotions. Shekhar sensed my reluctance and held my hand to assure me that we could face this challenge together. Yet, nothing prepared us for the ghastly sight that met our eyes when we entered the hall.

The ticket counter on the right side was full of soot, with pieces of broken glass scattered all around. Just behind the ticket counter was the car park, a sordid reminder of the inferno that had taken place three years ago. Charred, unclaimed cars and scooters stood there, as though they were still waiting for their owners to come and claim them. There were two transformers in the parking lot, and a Contessa car parked right outside the DVB transformer room was completely charred. The AC duct lay on the ground and the flooring held up by the joist was completely burnt. Electric cables dangled mid-air. The homeopathic dispensary located behind the transformer room was also completely gutted.

We had to grit our teeth and put up a courageous front. While the others were still on the ground floor, both of us rushed to the balcony. We could visualize how Unnati and Ujjwal must have suffered and died a very painful death. Since we knew their seat numbers we wanted to know where they had sat that fateful day. We were shocked to see that it was the first row on the right side, where the gangway and exit had been blocked. We realized that had the gangway and exit not been blocked, our children would have walked out of the hall safely.

As we stood next to their seats, we could not help but picture both of them struggling as the smoke engulfed the hall and trying to get out. The empty bottles of aerated drinks lying under their seats were a reminder that they must have been enjoying their beverages, unaware of what lay ahead of them. The strangest of thoughts kept playing on a loop in our heads. Did the children manage to move out of their seats or were they pushed around by the people around them because there was nobody to guide and help them? Shekhar kept repeating how he would have taken them out safely had he been there that day.

We stood there overcome by a deep and dreadful sense of guilt.

We were maddened by our grief, unable to control our feelings or our thoughts. What a painful death it must have been for both of them. Did they die while sitting in their seats? Which part of the balcony were their bodies found in? We were certain that they must have been together and holding each other's hands. For some time, we sat in their seats, holding hands, with tears rolling down our faces.

When Shekhar realized that the others were entering the balcony, he took charge of the situation. He held my hand and cautioned me to stay strong because we had a job to do. I cannot even begin to describe how hard it was for both of us to control our emotions, but we went with the commissioners to inspect the rest of the hall.

We were keen to go into the auditorium to see how the 750 patrons had managed to escape, while fifty-nine people perished and over 100 were injured, out of the 302 patrons seated in the balcony. Over there, we observed gangways on either side that directly led to the four exits located at the bottom of the screen. This explained how those patrons had managed to exit safely.

Every part of the theatre was a cruel reminder of the horrific incident. There were signs of struggle everywhere. Children's shoes, ladies' dupattas, salwars and broken bottles were scattered all over the balcony. The latches of the doors were broken. There was soot all over the walls. When we came out of the balcony to the lobby, we saw that it was almost completely destroyed. The door between the lobby and the staircase on the right was hanging off its hinges. Patrons who succeeded in coming out of the balcony after breaking open the door could not have accessed the staircase. The windowpanes had been broken using the huge metal ashtrays and benches. The situation in the toilets was equally pathetic. There were bloodstains and footprints all over the walls and the doors, as people must have injured themselves in their struggle to get out. Their last efforts were imprinted indelibly on Uphaar Cinema's body.

In the ladies' room, there were clothes scattered everywhere. Patrons had probably wet their clothes to cover their noses and mouths to avoid inhaling the poisonous gas. In the gents' toilet, the windowpanes were broken, probably in a desperate bid to escape.

This was nothing but a monument of mass murder. This sight haunts us even today and has been a constant reminder of the brutal killing of our lovely children.

When we came out of the hall, we were agitated and anguished. We knew that our children, and fifty-seven other people, had been brutally smothered to death. They could not possibly be at peace and neither could we. The AVUT members who had been waiting patiently outside met us with a barrage of questions. Was there no chance that our loved ones could have been saved? Why were they trapped in the balcony? How much did we think they might have suffered? Is it a fact that there was no gangway and an exit on one side of the balcony? Did we think they might have had a chance of survival had they been helped by the staff? Shekhar addressed these queries patiently, though his voice was choked with emotion. I was too disturbed to speak to any of the members.

After getting a detailed account of all the violations from Shekhar, the members were very agitated and angry. This visit only strengthened our resolve to ensure that the killers of our families were incarcerated.

We conferred among ourselves and took the decision to hold a havan and Shantipath for the peace of the departed souls at the Smriti Upavan memorial. We continue the same practice on 13 June every year, in the hope that our children will rest in peace.

On reaching home, we could not eat anything that night. We kept wondering how the Ansals had failed to provide a gangway and exit for the paying public, whereas they had ensured a separate entry/exit for each of the two private boxes built exclusively for their family and friends. After understanding the layout of the hall, we corroborated the same using technical reports, site plans and photographs to ensure that the defence counsel would not present distorted facts during the argument.

While awaiting the report of the commissioners, the High Court judgment on the maintainability of the writ was challenged in the Supreme Court by the Green Park Theatre Associated (P) Ltd—the company that owned Uphaar Cinema. Fortunately, this was dismissed on 17 August 2001. The Supreme Court did not interfere with the finding of the High Court. By now, four years had passed since the tragedy.

The commissioners finally submitted their report on 30 November 2001, nearly a year after the first visit to the hall. The commissioners claimed to have visited the theatre on several occasions. Their report pointed out fifty deviations and violations in the layout of the hall. The major ones were identical to those the Naresh Kumar inquiry report had highlighted and held as the main cause of the tragedy. Both the Naresh Kumar inquiry and the commissioners appointed by the Delhi High Court had come to almost identical conclusions.

The chief justice of the Delhi High Court constituted a special bench to hear our writ petition on a day-to-day basis. The arguments commenced in October 2001. Since I was well versed with the facts of the case, I decided to sit in the first row with my counsel to assist him. Many a time, the defence counsels asked me not to sit in the first row, but I never relented. This caused an objection to be raised by one of the defence counsels, who went on to suggest that he would never allow his clients to be seated in the front row. The judges understood the motive of the counsel, who was an eminent legal mind and, ironically, an acclaimed champion of human rights, and asked him not to be petty.

The writ petition was heard for nearly a year. All the parties advanced their arguments, blaming each other for the incident. None of the respondents were willing to accept responsibility for the tragedy. The counsel for the Ansals tried to negate the allegation made by AVUT regarding the many deviations from stipulated rules. AVUT also argued in court that the no objection certificates and the licences from the government agencies had been granted mechanically, without proper inspection of the hall as laid down in the Delhi Cinematograph Rules. Another point we emphasized was the installation of the DVB transformer in the parking lot. The contention of AVUT was that this was in total violation of the rules and by-laws framed for installation of such a transformer, and that it had been done with the consent and connivance of the owners so as to get favours from the DVB.

The contention of the Ansals' counsel was that the licensee had had no choice but to provide space for the installation of the DVB transformer. On the contrary, the DVB claimed that the tragedy had taken place due to complete and clear negligence on the part of the management of Uphaar Cinema. The management had been responsible for permitting/allowing parking in front of the transformer room, in an area of 16 feet that was actually earmarked as a manoeuvring space. The management stated that they had not instructed the parking attendant to permit any cars to be parked in front of the transformer room. There was provision for only fifteen cars here, but as many as twenty-eight cars had been parked there on 13 June 1997.

The DVB also accused the management of constructing a 12 foot parapet wall behind the transformer room, instead of a 3 foot wall, which had prevented the smoke from escaping the building.

The strategy of the Ansals' counsel was to ensure that they alone were not held responsible for the tragedy. In an attempt to save them, the counsel accused the DVB of improper maintenance of its transformer, and also accused the fire engines and ambulances of having arrived late and not being well equipped. The counsel went on to argue that the cinema hall had not been inspected by the authorities as per the prescribed safety norms. In an attempt to put across his arguments, he went on to compare the working of the government authorities of England to the authorities in India. He was trying to project a scenario where responsibility for the incident could be laid on the dereliction of duty on the part of various government agencies.

One of the judges asked the counsel to pause for a moment and consider what kind of damages the Ansals would have had to pay had this happened in England. Stumped by their question, the counsel was finally at a loss for words.

While the counsels for the Ansals were arguing in their defence, the judges put forth some queries. One of the judges asked the Ansals specifically why they had run away and not visited the injured and the families of the dead. To this, the counsel replied that the Ansals were scared that they might be lynched. Another question for which the counsel had no answer was why the Ansals had not offered even a paisa of ex gratia compensation to the victims and their families.

AVUT's writ petition had argued for the establishment of a trauma centre. The court directed the ministry of health to file an affidavit with regard to the status of the same. In compliance with the directions, the ministry of health and family welfare filed an affidavit on 9 January 2002, stating that in the meeting of the Cabinet Committee on Economic Affairs held in September 2001, the proposal for the setting up of an apex trauma centre at AIIMS, New Delhi, had been approved at an estimated cost of Rs 54.14 crore. The affidavit further stated that the implementation schedule for the trauma centre was to be thirty-three months. The High Court directed the Union of India to release funds earmarked for the project.

The judgment was reserved on 30 September 2002. A judgment is said to be reserved when the judges hearing a case decide that they require time to study evidence, the arguments and case law cited by the various parties.

In our case, the judges took nearly seven months for this purpose.

11

The Case Continues

The Delhi High Court pronounced its judgment on 24 April 2003. The court held that the fire had originated at the DVB transformer due to negligence in its maintenance. The fire would not have been so tragic had the cars not been parked right outside the transformer room and the exits not blocked to create a private box for the owners. The court also observed that had exits been located on both sides of the balcony, precious lives might have been saved as the patrons could have made their way outside the theatre quickly. The licensee (the owners) had committed statutory violations in order to obtain illegal profits. The licensing departments of the Delhi Police, Delhi Vidyut Board and Municipal Corporation of Delhi were all found guilty of contributory negligence due to their apathy and indifference to the critical matter of public safety.

The victims over the age of twenty years were awarded Rs 18 lakh each and victims under the age of twenty were awarded Rs 15 lakh each. The injured were awarded Rs 1 lakh each. Ansal Theatre and Clubotels (P) Ltd were liable to pay compensation to the extent of 55 per cent and each of the other respondents—the Delhi Vidyut Board, Licensing Authority of the Delhi Police and the Municipal Corporation of Delhi—would be liable to pay 15 per cent compensation. The court also directed Ansal Theatre and Clubotels (P) Ltd to pay Rs 2.5 crore as punitive damages, to be used for the setting up of the trauma centre. The High Court in its judgment also stated that the company would have no right to transfer, assign or create third-party rights in the cinema building. In case of non-payment of compensation within the period fixed by the court, the amount could be recovered by execution as decree through the sale of the cinema building or in another manner in accordance with the law.

The court held that it is the duty of the government to provide timely assistance to the victims of road or similar accidents, including fire. Despite the fact that a provision of more than Rs 50 crore had been sanctioned by the government for the setting up of a trauma service in the Ninth Five Year Plan and despite the fact that land had been made available for it since around 1988, no steps had been taken to set up a centralized trauma service. The court directed the Union of India to immediately set up this trauma centre. Thus, it was the Uphaar tragedy and the pain we suffered that catalysed the plan for the trauma centre. Thanks to the effort of AVUT members, Delhi now has the well-equipped Jai Prakash Apex Trauma Centre next to Safdarjung Hospital.

It is important to point out that this was the very first judgment to be delivered in our legal battle, and it completely corroborated all the points we had raised and argued for. Every other court of law upheld and reiterated the same conclusion this judgment had reached. And yet, despite our legal battles having continued for nineteen long years, our struggle still persists. If indeed, there is no disagreement in any court of law regarding the merits of the case, why have we had to wait for over nineteen years, and still have not received any closure?

The MCD, DCP (licensing) and DVB deposited their share of compensation in the High Court Registry as per the directions of the court. However, Ansal Theatre and Clubotels (P) Ltd moved an application, seeking more time to deposit the amount. They wanted the cinema building to be released to them. The application also stated that the amount could not be deposited unless the theatre was sold, since the company had no other source for discharging the liability determined by the court.

The High Court had also held that in the event of the Ansals not paying their part of the compensation within two months, the victims could recover the amount from the sale of Uphaar Cinema. We did not take this step in the interests of our case as Uphaar, in fact, held vital evidence that had to remain undisturbed.

The trial court had dismissed their application for the release of the cinema hall, so they moved a petition in the High Court. The Ansals pleaded that the cinema complex had been put to such disuse that it was ruined now. They further contended they had been virtually dispossessed of the property, which required maintenance and repair, and there would be no prejudice in the court if the cinema hall were to be released to them. In addition, they also took the stand that unless the property was released to them, they would not be in a position to discharge the liability towards the compensation ordered by the court.

Our counsel vehemently opposed the release of the cinema building to the Ansals, mainly on the grounds that unless the trial court inspected the premises properly, the scene of offence would have to be preserved.

The Ansals took this step with the sole aim of having the theatre released and erasing evidence that would prove vital for the case. The impact of the statements made by witnesses and the evidence could never be fully realized until the trial court could go and inspect the cinema premises, and it was essential that it remain untouched. The Ansals' application was fortunately dismissed by the High Court on 12 September 2003, with direction to the trial court that it may visit and inspect the hall if it decided to do so within one month, after concluding the examination of defence witnesses.

After the Ansals had declared in court that they had no property other than Uphaar Cinema to discharge their liability, we decided to have the files of Ansal Theatre and Clubotels (P) Ltd inspected at the Registrar of Companies (ROC). There was no Right to Information (RTI) Act those days and we had to manually inspect all the files. The parties were allowed to inspect them for only half an hour and hence, we had to make numerous visits to the ROC. We inspected the company's balance sheet and annual returns for various years and also examined other correspondence. We took photocopies of the documents and sought the help of a chartered accountant. We were startled to learn that the company not only owned Uphaar Cinema, but various other properties in Haryana and Uttar Pradesh with which they could have easily discharged their liability. The Ansals were projecting a false picture with the clear intention of getting the cinema back in order to make alterations and carry on with their profit-making business.

In September 2003, a special leave petition (SLP) was filed in the Supreme Court by the MCD and DCP (licensing) Delhi Police. Special leave petitions have been provided as a 'residual power' in the hands of the Supreme Court of India, to be exercised in cases when any substantial question of law is involved or gross injustice has been done. The court, while granting leave, stayed the disbursement of compensation to the victims deposited by the above parties in the registry of the Delhi High Court. This was a blow for the victims, especially those who had lost the only breadwinner of their families. Subsequently, in November 2003, the Ansals also filed an SLP. In August 2004, the Supreme Court asked AVUT to file a list of properties belonging to Ansal Theatre and Clubotels (P) Ltd from where the awarded amount could be recovered. However, the leave was granted in October 2004, after they were asked to deposit at least 50 per cent of the compensation amount awarded by the High Court. To deposit this amount, they sought the permission of the court to mortgage Uphaar Cinema, since they claimed that they had no other source to discharge their liability. The same was granted by the Supreme Court with directions that for the purpose of arranging funds, the company could offer the cinema building as security and raise money from the financial institution to the tune of Rs 3,01,40,000. Furthermore, they could not create any other encumbrance. The court also directed that as per the order of the criminal court, the sealing of the property and maintaining the same intact till the criminal trial is over would be meticulously observed.

Although it is impossible for anyone to believe that the Ansals did not have enough money to pay their dues, they were given the benefit of the doubt and were able once again to exercise partial control over the theatre.

Once leave was granted, the matter remained pending in the Supreme Court for almost six years.

We were quite optimistic that, considering the gravity of the tragedy, the Supreme Court would dispose of the appeals in the shortest possible time. Therefore, we were surprised when the matter was not scheduled for a hearing. We made inquiries about the procedure for the appeal and the amount of time it usually takes. We learnt then that it takes years before an appeal is taken up for hearing due to the pendency of cases. We decided to forget about our civil matter and concentrate on the criminal matter, which was anyway more important for us. Our focus shifted back to the criminal case, but there was no relief for us from court proceedings. It took more than six years for the appeal to be heard for final disposal.

The whole process delayed the disbursement of compensation to the victims. AVUT moved two applications for early hearing, but they were both dismissed by the court. It was only when AVUT moved the third application for early hearing in May 2009 that the matter was taken up for final disposal in November that year.

During the arguments, the licensee argued that the entire liability should be placed upon the DVB. It was contended that the DVB had installed a transformer of 1000 KV capacity without obtaining the statutory sanction/approval and providing all the safety measures it was duty-bound to, under the relevant Electricity Rules. The contention of the Ansals was what could be awarded as a public law remedy is only a nominal interim or palliative compensation and if any claimants (legal heirs of the deceased or any injured) sought a higher compensation, they should file a suit for recovery thereof. It was contended that the High Court could not have assumed the monthly income of each adult who died as being not less than Rs 15,000 per month and that determining the compensation by applying the multiplier of fifteen was improper.

During the course of the hearing, the court had asked the counsel for the Ansals what amount of compensation they considered justified. The counsel promptly replied that the compensation should not be more than Rs 5 lakh per deceased person and the court made a note of the same.

On the last day of the hearing, 16 December 2009, the additional solicitor general appearing for the Licensing Authority/Central government submitted that the share of compensation deposited by the DCP (licensing) should be dispersed as ex gratia to the victims. The court accepted the same and passed directions accordingly.

The Ansals' counsel too offered to deposit a sum of Rs 4 crore on behalf of the family. Of this, Rs 3 crore was intended for disbursement to the victims and Rs 1 crore as the family's contribution towards the trauma centre at AIIMS. The offer of Rs 1 crore was rejected by the Supreme Court, stating that 'it appears that you want to evoke this court's sympathy for you'. AVUT's counsel submitted that the families of the victims were not interested in accepting any payment from the theatre owners or their family as charity or ex gratia, and they would receive compensation from the theatre owners only in accordance with the court's direction. He also asked that they not intimidate the witnesses and tamper with the court records.

It is worth mentioning here that a day before the judgment of our civil appeal was pronounced, that is on 12 October 2011, I received a telephone call from a journalist whose identity I am unable to share. He informed me that the judgment would be delivered the next day. He also informed me that while he had been in the court, a legal luminary appearing on behalf of Sushil Ansal in the criminal appeal chose to be present in the courtroom of the presiding judge who had heard our civil appeal, and informed him that he should be careful in delivering the judgment in our case, as it would have major repercussions on other ongoing criminal appeals.

The judgment for the civil appeal was finally pronounced on 13 October 2011. The Supreme Court, while upholding the findings of the High Court, held that had the parapet wall not been raised to the roof level, the fumes from the fire would have dispersed. If one of the exits from the balcony had not been blocked by the illegal construction of an owner's box, and if the gangway had not been closed to make space for additional seats, visitors in the balcony could have easily dispersed through the gangway and exited using the staircase that was unaffected by the smoke. Had the cars not been parked in the immediate vicinity of the transformer room and the required pit constructed to drain the transformer oil, the oil would not have leaked into the passage. Neither would the burning oil have lit the cars in the parking lot, as the fire would have been restricted to the transformer room. If even one of the three causes for which the theatre owner was responsible had been avoided, the calamity would not have taken place.

The court further observed that none of the patrons seated in the main hall died. Those on the second floor of the building too escaped. It was only those in the balcony who choked on the noxious fumes and died of asphyxiation. Their deaths were due to negligence and greed on the part of the licensee. While holding the licensee and the DVB responsible, the court exonerated MCD and the Licensing Authority. Of the total compensation to be paid to the victims, the licensee had to pay 85 per cent and the DVB 15 per cent.

The court further observed the need for comprehensive legislation dealing with tortious liability of the state, whose instrumentalities had been highlighted by the Supreme Court. Due to a lack of legislation, the courts dealing with such cases had not followed a uniform pattern. The court also observed that no legislation had been enacted to deal with such situations despite the concern shown by the apex court.

In a sense, this would appear to be an open admission of the very lapses in the legal system that led to such havoc and loss of life.

Despite these findings, the compensation awarded by the High Court was reduced to Rs 10 lakh to the victims above the age of twenty and Rs 7.5 lakh to those below the age of twenty. If this amount is converted into dollars it amounts to approximately \$14,687 and \$11,015 respectively. The Supreme Court also reduced the punitive damages from Rs 2.5 crore to Rs 25 lakh for the trauma centre payable by the Ansals to the Union of India. We've given the figures in dollars for the reader to understand how compensation works across the world.

We were appalled by this decision. The reason for slashing the compensation was that the Supreme Court felt the Delhi High Court had erred in calculating the damage on the basis of an income of Rs 15,000 per month of each adult on the grounds that they belonged to a higher income group since they had bought a balcony ticket to watch the movie.

The Supreme Court, in its judgment, gave the liberty to the legal representative of the deceased to approach the High Court in case they were not satisfied with the compensation amount. They were permitted to file an application for compensation with supporting documentary proof (to show the age and income) before the registrar general. However, members of AVUT unanimously decided not to approach the High Court for any further compensation because ours had never been a fight for monetary gains. No amount of compensation could alleviate our pain at the loss of our loved ones or redress the emotional loss suffered by the victims' families. The reason we filed the writ petition had been to create a precedent for the speedy and uniform dispensation of compensation after such man-made disasters, which would, we hoped, act as a deterrent for future occurrences. Sadly, we had failed in our endeavour.

By now, we knew that going back to the High Court for the summary inquiry would result in the chain of delays and hurdles that we had encountered since the start of our legal journey.

It is also pertinent to mention here that the DVB had not challenged the High Court's verdict of bringing down the quantum of compensation. They had deposited their share of compensation to be disbursed to the victims in June 2003. However, the Supreme Court, while delivering the final verdict reduced their payable share. This meant that instead of paying 15 per cent of Rs 15 lakh and Rs 18 lakh each as awarded by the High Court, the DVB was now required to pay 15 per cent, i.e., Rs 7.5 lakh and Rs 10 lakh each. However, their payment had already been disbursed to the legal heirs of the victims. Despite the fact that the DVB had not challenged the compensation in the first place, the Supreme Court judgment now warranted that the additional amount paid by the DVB be adjusted against the compensation to be paid by the Ansals. Once again, the victims were at a disadvantage.

Our endeavour had been to demand and help establish a culture of accountability, and make the law-enforcing agencies more responsible. We believed that this judgment would send the wrong signals to the perpetrators. It was our belief that the Supreme Court had lost an opportunity to lay down guidelines that would ensure greater safety in public spaces.

While exonerating the MCD and the Licensing Authority with regard to monetary liability, the Supreme Court had observed that they had performed their duties in a mechanical, casual and lackadaisical manner. The courts should have made them liable to pay heavy compensation so that authorities would be deterred from compromising on safety norms in the future. We failed to comprehend why the courts would be lenient towards the agencies, especially since it was so clear that there was a nexus between them, the owners and occupiers of the concerned public space. To us, this seemed like a blanket assurance to agencies that no matter what they did or however much they endangered the public by not respecting the set guidelines, the law would be there to protect them. After all, it is these very departments who educate the owners of the spaces on how to subvert the rules and by-laws in exchange for monetary consideration.

The larger concern is how could such a conservative judgment act as a deterrent in the future? The answer is negative. Today, most public spaces are run and managed by big corporates. When they know that the compensation requirements are so paltry, we cannot expect them to deter from violating safety norms and thus endangering human lives. We were also amazed that after holding the company liable to pay 85 per cent of the compensation amount, the Supreme Court had reduced the amount. There is no justification for this as the world over compensation is decided by the court on the basis of the paying capacity of the individual or the company. Such a lenient judgment only encourages the owners and occupiers to compromise on safety rules and endanger human lives.

The only silver lining of the judgment was that the theatre owners were held 85 per cent liable for the tragedy, in agreement with what we had been saying since 1997. With this judgment, the corporate sector would be brought under the ambit of Article 226 of the Constitution of India, and would be liable to pay compensation and punitive damages in case of any man-made disaster in public spaces managed and run by them.

While affirming several suggestions made by the High Court, the Supreme Court added the following suggestions to the government for consideration and implementation:

- Every licensee (cinema theatre) shall be required to draw up an emergency evacuation plan and get it approved by the Licensing Authority.
- Every cinema theatre shall be required to screen a short documentary during every show showing the exits, emergency escape routes and instructions as to what to do and what not to do in the case of fire or other hazards.
- The staff/ushers in every cinema theatre should be trained in fire drills and evacuation procedures to provide support to the patrons in case of fire or other calamity.
- While the theatres are entitled to regulate the exit through doors other than the entry door, under no circumstances, the entry door (which can act as an emergency exit) in the event of fire or other emergency should be bolted from outside. At the end of the show, the ushers may request the patrons to use the exit doors by placing a temporary barrier across the entry gate which should be easily movable.
- There should be mandatory half-yearly inspections of cinema theatres by a senior officer from the Delhi Fire Services, electrical inspectorate and the Licensing Authority to verify whether the electrical installations and safety measures are properly functioning and take action wherever necessary.

- As the cinema theatres have undergone a change in the last decade with more and more multiplexes coming up, separate rules should be made for multiplex cinemas whose requirements and concerns are different from stand-alone cinema theatres.
- An endeavour should be made to have a single point nodal agency/Licensing Authority consisting of experts in structural engineering/building, fire prevention, electrical systems, etc. The existing system of police granting licences should be abolished.
- Each cinema theatre, whether a multiplex or stand-alone theatre, should be given a fire safety rating by the Fire Services which can be in green (fully compliant), yellow (satisfactorily compliant) or red (poor compliance). The rating should be prominently displayed in each theatre so that there is awareness among the patrons and building owners.
- The Delhi Disaster Management Authority, established by the Government of the NCT of Delhi, may expeditiously evolve standards to manage the disasters relating to cinema theatres and the guidelines in regard to ex gratia assistance. It should be directed to conduct mock drills in each cinema theatre at least once a year.

It has been over five years since the judgment was pronounced, but the government and its instrumentalities have not even considered implementing the recommendations given by the highest court of the land. This shows the lack of will in our administration while dealing with public safety.

The years after the incident were very demanding. After the murder of our children, we had struggled to come to terms with our grief and loss. Though their absence and the pain have been our constant companion, we learnt to deliberately concentrate on the task of seeking and getting justice for them. But constant reminders of the deep-rooted corruption in our systems and the tragic fact that we as a society do not value human life often affected our resolve and determination. Dealing with various court cases was a full-time job, full of new obstacles and challenges due to the various applications moved by the accused to delay the proceedings. Left alone without any moral support from friends or family, both of us realized that we only had each other's shoulders to cry on. Our business took a back seat as we were too involved in the cases to attend to our work fully. A sense of pessimism and cynicism had set in as the cases were not proceeding towards any conclusion.

There were times when we both wondered if we would be alive to take the cases to their logical end. We wished we could turn the clock back. There were times when we thought of how our lives would have been had our dreams not been so cruelly destroyed. Wouldn't Unnati have reached marriageable age by now, we sometimes asked ourselves. Who would she have wanted to marry, if at all, and what kind of marriage would she and her companion have wanted? Perhaps we would have even become grandparents by now. All parents think of such moments and look forward to them. For us, the tragedy is that we remain parents even now and cannot help thinking of such milestones that were cruelly snatched away from us. But we do not have words to describe the torture we experience each time we think of these special moments, because we are reminded that such pleasures are not for us.

Back home after a long day in court, both of us were preparing for the next day's hearing. At about 8 p.m. the doorbell rang; Shekhar opened the door to find one of Unnati's close friends standing outside. He had come to invite us for his wedding, armed with a box of sweets and his wedding card. For a few moments we were speechless, but Shekhar took control of his emotions first and congratulated him, promising him that we would attend his wedding. We were both very happy for him, but after he left we both sat in silence, without exchanging a word. We could not help imagining that had Unnati been alive, we could have been preparing for her wedding too. But that was not meant to be. Try as we might we could not control the pain we felt. Unable to continue working, we decided to call it a day. The eerie silence that descended in the house both haunted us and mocked us. We could only hear the clock ticking away indicating that time moves on, but for us life had become stagnant. We knew that Unnati would have wanted us to attend her friend's wedding, but we couldn't gather the courage to do so.

12

Little Compensation

We failed in our endeavour to ensure a uniform and heavy compensation to the victims of the Uphaar fire tragedy. There are several instances to show that courts in other countries deal sternly and swiftly with tragedies involving human lives, and award heavy compensation and punitive damages to the victims and survivors. Oil giant BP reached an $18.7 billion settlement with the US Department of Justice following the 2010 Gulf of Mexico oil spill. Nearly $175 million in settlement was paid to the families of the victims of the Station nightclub fire in the United States, which killed around 100 people and injured 200. In the recent ferry accident in South Korea, a compensation of $3,80,000 was paid to each of the 250 students who died or were declared missing.

In September 2008, a former Supreme Court judge claimed heavy compensation from a leading English news channel, which inadvertently used his photo instead of that of another judge allegedly involved in a provident fund scam. The district court of Pune ordered the channel to pay damages to the tune of Rs 100 crore to the aggrieved judge. The Bombay High Court admitted the appeal, but refused to grant a stay on the execution of the degree. The news channel was asked to deposit Rs 20 crore in six weeks and a bank guarantee of Rs 80 crore in another ten weeks as a precondition for hearing the appeal. An SLP was filed in the Supreme Court against the High Court order, but the apex court refused to interfere. The speed with which this case was decided shows that the courts can act swiftly if they need to. The suit was filed on 13 November 2008 and the judgment delivered on 26 April 2011. It goes to show how insignificant a common man's life is when compared to the dignity of a former judge.

In another incident, a former judge of the Madras High Court, who missed a flight due to the negligence of the airline's ground staff, was awarded compensation of Rs 5 lakh for the mental agony he had to undergo. The State Consumer Forum also asked the airline to refund his airfare of Rs 4682. This incident occurred on 28 April 2010 and relief was granted on 30 January 2012.

The reason for citing these examples is to show the disparity in the time taken for victims or petitioners to be compensated. In the case of a man-made disaster like the Uphaar fire, which shook the nation's conscience, it took fourteen years for the families of the victims to be compensated, while the same was provided in a mere two to three years when it involved judges being subject to human error.

Interestingly, just after the Uphaar verdict in December 2011, the Supreme Court awarded a compensation of Rs 13.48 lakh to an elephant hit by a Kerala State Road Transport Corporation bus. We are respectful of the rights of all living beings, but this verdict proves beyond doubt that in the eyes of the courts, human life is cheaper than that of an animal's.

In a case involving medical negligence, the Supreme Court awarded a compensation of Rs 6 crore in October 2013 to one Dr Saha for the death of his wife. In comparison, a total compensation of Rs 6.50 crore was awarded to the Uphaar victims. What we have been unable to come to terms with is the disparity in compensation given to the legal heirs of those who died due to different forms of negligence, be it medical or any other negligence. All this while, we had assumed that all lives have equal value in the eyes of justice, but our courts have proven otherwise.

The purpose of our filing the writ petition was to ensure uniform compensation and speedy relief for any man-made tragedies in the future. But unfortunately, it took us fourteen long years to get a final judgment from the apex court. We were fortunate that we could sustain our efforts for such a long period of time, thanks to being represented pro bono by K.T.S. Tulsi and his team of lawyers. It is a well-known fact that cases take decades to reach their logical conclusion in Indian courts and the expenses involved while engaging a good, senior lawyer are often well beyond the reach of an ordinary citizen.

13

We Lost Nineteen Years, They Lost Six Months

Criminal law provides the provision for prescribing punishment to those who endanger the life, property, safety and welfare of others. The sole purpose of this is to punish the perpetrators of crime. The main purpose of criminal law is to ensure timely justice, so that the aggrieved party does not indulge in any revenge-seeking vigilantism. Criminal law also ensures that no innocent is incarcerated if he has not committed a crime. It gives an opportunity for reformation, reconciliation and rehabilitation of criminals back into mainstream society.

The purpose of punishment is to act as a deterrent—by punishing criminals, the state hopes to dissuade people from committing crimes in the future. The main intent behind the incarceration of criminals is to prevent the individual from committing another crime, allowing him to reform.

India follows an adversarial system of justice, where the onus of proof is on the state (the prosecution) to prove its case against the accused, and until and unless the accusations are proved beyond reasonable doubt, he/she is presumed innocent.

The general perception people hold about our criminal justice system is based on its representation in films. But, in reality, the criminal procedure in India is very cumbersome and there are many stages of trial before the case actually reaches its conclusion. We are not lawyers and, hence, we were not aware of the nuances of each of these stages, but we learnt about them when we started attending the court proceedings regularly. We have gathered from this experience that it is imperative that a litigant knows what to expect when he approaches the court to get justice. Therefore, we are enumerating the various stages of the criminal trial in order to give our readers an insight into India's criminal justice system.

- Registration of the first information report (FIR). It is a written document prepared by the police when they receive information about the commission of a cognizable offence.
- The investigating agency commences the investigation and starts collecting evidence. During this stage, the accused can be arrested by the investigating agency and produced before the magistrate within twenty-four hours of arrest.
- After a thorough investigation, if the investigating agency finds that there is enough prima facie evidence (a fact presumed to be true unless it is disproved), a charge sheet is filed in the court. In the absence of sufficient evidence, the investigating agency files a closure report in the concerned court. The charge sheet is a brief summary of how an offence has been committed, the role of each person involved in the crime and the sections under which the investigating officer has charged all the accused. The charge sheet

also contains the names of the prosecution witnesses, relevant documents, circumstantial evidence, and expert and scientific evidence relied upon by the investigating agency. Filing of the charge sheet generally means that the investigation in the case is complete. It is for the court to take cognizance of the evidence collected by the investigating agency. During the course of the trial, if new facts emerge, the agency may file additional charge sheets.

- Once the court takes cognizance of the case, all the accused are supplied copies of the police report and other documents relied upon by the prosecuting agency under section 207 of the Code of Criminal Procedure (CrPC).

- If the case is triable by a court of session, without delay and free of cost, the magistrate supplies all the documents and statements of the witnesses to the accused, and commits the case to the court of session under section 209 of the CrPC.

- The framing of charges under section 228 of the CrPC involves the sessions court looking into the evidence collected by the investigating agency and applying its mind to the charges under which an accused has to be booked. If, prima facie, there is enough evidence, charges are framed by the court. If the accused pleads guilty, the court decides the punishment accordingly. If the accused pleads not guilty, he is informed of the charges under which he would be required to face trial. If the judge finds that there is not enough evidence against the accused, he/she is discharged. The court has to record the reasons for discharging the accused.

- After the framing of charges, the prosecution is required to produce the prosecution witnesses and all the evidence collected by them before the court. The process of recording the statements of the witnesses by the prosecutor is called the examination-in-chief. The documentary evidence used by the prosecution must be exhibited by the concerned witnesses; this sort of evidence is called an exhibit. The witnesses produced by the prosecution are expected to support the case presented by them and if they fail to do so, they are declared hostile. The defence is entitled to cross-examine these witnesses, so they are able to locate any discrepancies in their statements and thus bolster their own case.

- Section 313 of the CrPC empowers the court to ask for an explanation from the accused personally, in order to explain any circumstances appearing in the evidence against him. After the prosecution witnesses have been examined, and before the accused is called to his defence, the court questions him/her generally with regard to the case. The basic idea is to give an opportunity to the accused to be heard and explain the facts and circumstances appearing in the evidence against him. Under this section, the accused shall not be administered an oath and the accused may refuse to answer the questions. The answers given by the accused may be taken into consideration in such an inquiry or trial, and used as evidence for or against him.

- After the statement of the accused, the defence is given an opportunity to present any evidence in his/her support. The defence can also produce its witnesses who may be cross-examined by the prosecution. These are called defence witnesses.

- After the defence presents its evidence, the prosecution is called for its final arguments in the case. Here, the prosecution generally sums up its case against the accused. After this, the defence also presents its final arguments. The court then reserves its judgment.

- After hearing all the arguments, the judge delivers a final judgment either holding the accused guilty or acquitting him/her. If a person is convicted for a particular offence, then a date is fixed for the arguments on the sentence.

- Once a person is convicted, both sides present their arguments on the quantum of punishment that should be awarded.

- After the arguments on sentencing, the court finally decides on the punishment for the accused.

The most arduous task ahead of us was to follow up on the criminal trial. The Indian criminal justice system is heavily loaded against the victims and favours the accused, especially if the accused are rich, powerful and corrupt. Since the Ansals come from a very influential section of society, they were willing to go to any length to delay and derail the trial. They were being represented not by one or two lawyers, but a battery of high-profile, competent lawyers. On the other hand, the victims, that is us in this case, were being represented by a public prosecutor engaged by the CBI, whose profile was certainly lower than the Ansals' team of lawyers. Thus, we were at a disadvantage.

During the committal stage of the criminal trial in the court of the magistrate, the defence counsels sought adjournments on the grounds that they had not been supplied with the complete set of documents used by the prosecuting agency. We sought legal advice to understand why the case was not progressing and were told that under section 207 of the CrPC, the accused have to be furnished with all the documents that the prosecution relies upon in the case, as well as the statements of witnesses. We were also told it was a minor procedure, which should not take more than two to three hearings. But the problem persisted for over a year.

The counsels for the Ansals also moved an application for separating the trial as the accused had been charged under different sections of the Indian Penal Code. This request was turned down by the magistrate.

In October 1998, the accused filed an application for the release of Uphaar Cinema so that they could proceed with their business. This application too was dismissed by the magistrate. When the court was scheduling the next date of hearing, the lawyers wanted a date after Diwali, stating it was the festival season and they wanted to spend time with their families. The lawyers and the accused exchanged greetings while leaving the courtroom, oblivious of the fact that the families of the victims were present in the courtroom.

Shekhar and I were transported back to how we used to celebrate Diwali with Unnati and Ujjwal. The children always looked forward to the festival with a lot of excitement and were very enthusiastic about shopping for the occasion. Our house used to be brightly lit and we were always joined by a lot of family and friends for the celebration. We do not look forward to Diwali any more, or any other cause for celebration for that matter—birthdays, anniversaries, festivals, etc., only depress us further. They are constant reminders that we have little to celebrate and no one to celebrate with. We can only wish the children were with us to celebrate. As we left the courtroom that day, it was difficult for us to keep our emotions and tears under control until we could get some privacy.

Around this time, during one of the hearings, the leading defence counsel for the Ansals had the temerity to call the tragedy an act of god. He even compared the fire to the

Bhopal gas tragedy and blatantly asked why such a hue and cry was being created when, after all, only fifty-nine lives were lost. Over the years, our continuing battle for justice had prepared us to face bruising events at every turn, but, at that juncture, when we were relatively new to the ways of the court and the pain, we could not express the sense of outrage and shock we experienced on hearing this dastardly argument. Imagine how distressed we were to hear that our loved ones were being referred to as mere numbers! We wondered how this could be called an act of god.

Unable to control ourselves, we tried addressing the court ourselves, but were rebuked by the defence counsels, who stated that we have no locus standi (the right or capacity to bring an action or to appear in a court). On making inquiries about our role in the criminal trial, we were told that as victims, we could engage a lawyer, but he could not extend his role beyond assisting the public prosecutor, and only if the prosecutor were agreeable to it. We realized then that this is a major drawback in the system. The urgent need for a public prosecutor who was competent, could match the wisdom of the defence counsels, and, if required, outmanoeuvre them, became starkly apparent to us.

Our counsel advised us to be vigilante litigants and ensure that we schedule a conference with the arguing lawyer a day before our matter was listed. In one of his initial meetings with us, Tulsi referred to an old Hindi proverb, *muddai sust gavaah chust*, which means: witness active, defendant inactive. He was warning us that we needed to be alert all the time, and never lose our momentum and intensity.

We were now faced with the question of who would spare the time to follow up on the cases, both civil and criminal, on behalf of AVUT. Shekhar and I decided that we would follow up the cases between us, since we had decided to dedicate our lives to getting justice for our children. Moreover, we had realized that this was especially relevant in the criminal trial, as it would be the state that represented the victims.

We understood early on that it was not enough to merely attend the court proceedings. The need of the hour was to coordinate closely with the CBI to ensure proper progress in the case. We met senior officers of the CBI and requested them to expedite the process of furnishing documents to the accused, and also appoint a special public prosecutor so that we would be well represented.

The case was finally committed to the sessions court on 4 January 1999. This whole process took thirty hearings. Normally, the simple clerical process of making copies of documents to be provided to each of the accused should not take more than two to three hearings. As we have mentioned earlier, it took thirty hearings in our case. Delays were created on the basis of the most flimsy excuses—sometimes, photographs included in the evidence were declared not clear enough, while at other times the documents and the site plans of Uphaar Cinema were declared to be illegible.

During our initial visits to court, we were just silent spectators. The matter would be heard in court only for a few minutes and the session would be adjourned for one reason or the other. We realized that to fight a legal battle, we would have to be actively involved in the case and understand the court proceedings. It was not enough to merely attend the sessions; it was vital to understand what was being presented. As the courts were very crowded, the arguments advanced by the lawyers were inaudible and hence, we could not understand what had transpired. It became imperative for us to familiarize ourselves with the court environment and proceedings. We decided to reach the court early to stand in front to understand what was being argued.

The most frequently used terms were CrPC, IPC and IEA. We were not familiar with the legal language and were handicapped by our ignorance. We sought help from lawyers to understand the same and learnt that Indian criminal laws are divided into three major Acts: the Code of Criminal Procedure, 1973 (CrPC), the Indian Penal Code, 1960 (IPC), and the Indian Evidence Act, 1872 (IEA). We bought the *Criminal Manual* to understand the above acts better.

The CrPC lays down the procedure to be followed by the courts for a criminal case. The IPC is the primary penal law of India, which is applicable to all offences. The IEA contains a set of rules and allied issues governing the admissibility of evidence in Indian courts of law. We tried to familiarize ourselves with the legal terminology used in the criminal manual, but there were hiccups to begin with. The exposure we received in the courts helped us understand and interpret the sections of the code.

Apart from the criminal code, the counsels referred to various statutes like the Cinematograph Act and Rules, Building By-laws, Electricity Rules, Fire Safety Act and Rules, which governed the cinema halls. We found the statute book easier to understand than the *Criminal Manual*.

However, understanding all this was not an easy task and sometimes we felt as though we were preparing for a competitive examination. There were more challenges ahead when counsels for the Ansals started referring to the site plans. Although we had visited Uphaar innumerable times to watch films, we were not familiar with the layout of the cinema complex. After seeing the site plans, we realized that they were too complicated for us to understand and we decided to seek help from an architect. The architect compared the plans approved by the MCD with the eventual layout of the cinema hall as on 13 June 1997. He apprised us of the many deviations in the structure. To understand things better, we compared the site plans with the photographs of each floor of the building submitted by the Central Forensic Science Laboratory (CFSL). We also took the help of the expert committee reports by the MCD and PWD listing floor-wise deviations. While going through the reports one of the most glaring deviations we observed was that the balcony had 302 seats as opposed to 250 seats originally sanctioned in 1973 by the MCD. This exercise helped us understand the various structural deviations and violations in the cinema complex.

When the counsels were arguing on the question of law, they referred to judgments of the higher courts. We noted the judgments cited by the defence counsels and left it to our counsels to interpret them because we did not have access to the judgments. It was only after reading the judgments delivered on the maintainability in our civil matter and the judgment with regard to the compensation by the High Court that we started understanding and interpreting them. By 2000, we had familiarized ourselves with legal terminology and this helped us immensely. Once the judgments were available online, we went through each and every one of them that had been cited by the defence counsels in the criminal matter to prepare ourselves for conferences with our counsels, where we put across our points with clarity and effectiveness.

The next step was the framing of the charges under section 228 of the CrPC. The matter was assigned to the additional sessions judge who recused himself from the case on the grounds that one of the accused was known to him. The case was then allocated to another judge, who heard the matter from 10 March 1999 onwards. When the matter was being argued, we were not satisfied with the presentation of the case by the public prosecutor. Being an old-timer, he wrote his notes in Urdu before putting them across to the judge. On many occasions, several crucial details were left out. This was a matter of grave concern for us. We decided to assist him in the matter, but he was dismissive of our efforts.

The matter was progressing at a snail's pace. The counsel for the CBI moved an application for day–to-day hearing of the matter, but it was rejected by the additional sessions judge. The CBI and thirteen out of the sixteen accused had concluded their arguments on the charges. The judge adjudicating the matter was transferred after thirty-six hearings and the matter was assigned to another judge on 10 January 2000. This was a sheer waste of judicial time and a setback for the victims' families. Why is it that while transferring judges who are adjudicating such sensitive matters, the concerned administrative officer does not deliberate on the delay the transfer might cause and the toll it will take on the victims? The courts are supposed to proceed with cases and expedite the process of a trial. However, such administrative hurdles do nothing but delay due process.

When the High Court transfers a judge who is listening to sensitive matters, it should lay down certain guidelines. We tried to bring this to the notice of the chief justice of the High Court and sent him a letter of appeal asking him to take into account the inordinate delay that would be caused by the timing of the transfer, but we received no response.

As if this was not enough, during the course of the hearing, a tenant of Uphaar Cinema moved an application for the release of the building, so she could conduct her business. This request was rejected by the court. After the hearing, while we were coming out of the courtroom, the tenant accosted me and asked why, being a mother, I was not sitting at home and mourning the death of my children. Why had I sent my children alone to watch a movie that day? Shocked and taken aback by her callous behaviour, we thought we were witnessing a freak incident and chose to focus on the case instead. What we did not realize was that this was just the beginning of our ordeal and that we would be subjected to the worst of experiences over the course of the next nineteen years.

The matter was now listed for hearing before the newly appointed additional sessions judge and the hearing commenced afresh. But the public prosecutor suddenly withdrew from the case on the grounds of ill health, without informing the prosecuting agency. Once again, this was a huge problem as it is a long-drawn process to get a special public prosecutor appointed, as he/she would have to be approved by the concerned ministry. We apprised the joint director of the CBI on the state of affairs and requested him to appoint another special public prosecutor. The process was initiated and this time we took a personal interest in the matter. We also interacted with the government to expedite the appointment.

After the appointment of the next public prosecutor for the case, we had to be very vigilant to ensure no evidence was left out of the hearing. This demanded a lot of patience and perseverance. We had to sit through prolonged court hearings, make copious notes, brief the press and ensure that Uphaar did not end up forgotten and brushed under the carpet, like many other man-made disasters.

The case documents ran to over 40,000 pages, but we decided to go through each and every one of them to help us assist the public prosecutor better. On studying the various expert opinions, we realized that every rule in the book had been violated and there were innumerable deviations in the building which had resulted in the catastrophe. To come to this conclusion, we had to study the Cinematograph Rules, Building By-laws, Fire Safety Rules and Electricity Rules in minute detail. Hence, we decided that between us, Shekhar would go through the Acts and Rules, and I would go through the statements of witnesses and the documents. By familiarizing ourselves with the documents and the statutes, we were able to assist the prosecutor and our counsels effectively. Since the fire had originated from the transformer, it was imperative for us to understand how a transformer works to begin with. We sought the help of an electrical engineer. We took the reports of the Central Forensic Science Laboratory and the electrical inspector, and the photographs of the damaged transformer to him. After scrutinizing all the material, he explained what happened on that fateful day. He made us familiar with the different parts of the transformer and their functions. This exercise helped us understand the technical arguments put forth by the counsels of the DVB and the Ansals.

We also went through all the eyewitness accounts to understand what had happened inside the hall. We were not trained lawyers who could read such statements in a detached manner and sift through the material to find what was relevant to the case. This was, for us, one of the most excruciatingly painful experiences, because we had to go through the statements of each of the witnesses given to the prosecuting agency (under section 161 of the CrPC). These were the people who had escaped from the hall. While reading the statements for the first time, we could not help but visualize how our children might have suffered and struggled to escape. We could not stop the tears from rolling down our cheeks and we kept the statements aside, determined never to read them again.

14

The Trial Continues

We could not stick to our decision with regard to the witness statements for very long. When we heard the defence counsels selectively read out only those portions of the statements that would help them, it became imperative for us to go through them once again, despite the trauma we knew we would have to undergo. As bereaved parents, we had to control our emotions and read the statements from a lawyer's perspective in order to gain clear understanding of the entire incident. Though this was a torturous experience, it had to be done. Today, after the passage of many years, we do not regret having done this, since it helped immensely in our understanding of the incident. It also helped during the trial when the eyewitnesses deposed in court.

Each day, we gained more insights into the facts of the case and began understanding the arguments advanced by the prosecution as well as the defence. We realized that only a select portion of the statements, reports and rules were being cited by the defence lawyers and used to interpret the situation to their advantage. This was done to mislead the courts. Since we had studied each and every document, we made notes and assisted the prosecution in countering their arguments.

Even the gatekeeper of the cinema hall was being represented by one of the leading lawyers of the Patiala House Courts. It was an open fact that the fees of the lawyers representing the cinema staff were being paid by the Ansals. An application was moved on behalf of the gatekeeper in February 2000 for the appointment of an amicus curiae, stating that he did not have the money to pay the lawyer's fee. Amicus curiae refers to a friend of the court, who is generally appointed to provide free legal aid to indigent or needy persons. Noting the attitude of the defence counsels, the CBI moved an application for a day-to-day trial, to which the defence raised an objection. However, the judge decided to hear the matter twice a week. (*Indian Express*, 12 February 2000)

Things were further delayed when the Bar Association went on strike and the hearing could not take place for almost two months. (*Dainik Jagran*, 15 May 2000) In May 2000, applications were moved on behalf of the two managers of the cinema hall on grounds similar to that of the gatekeeper—for appointment of an amicus curiae. It was during the course of this argument that the leading lawyers of the managers, who were also responsible officers in the Bar Association, insisted that they be paid as much as a special public prosecutor appointed by the CBI. (*The Hindu*, 25 May 2000)This request was turned down. It was another attempt to interfere with the administration of justice, made more obvious because the same lawyers continued appearing for the managers and gatekeeper for over a decade.

We were also subjected to a lot of humiliation during the court proceedings. Offensive, derogatory and humiliating comments were hurled at us repeatedly by the defence counsels, the Ansals' staff and their security staff. Though this was done to intimidate us and deter us from attending court regularly, the hostile atmosphere only made us more determined to succeed. Since various cases were pending in different courts, there were times when Shekhar could not accompany me to the trial court. Each time I visited the courts alone, the security staff of the Ansals would pass obscene remarks like '*Kutiya phir se aa gayi hai.* (The bitch is here again.)'

Since there was no security in the courts, the Ansals were accompanied by gun-toting security guards. I brought this fact to the notice of the judge. On being questioned about it, the counsel for the Ansals denied my allegations. However, the judge issued a warning to the Ansals. This did not stop the security guards from blocking my way into the courtroom and passing derogatory comments.

I also realized that my resolve for justice only grew stronger every time the Ansals, their lawyers or their staff tried to threaten or humiliate me, and I continued to attend court proceedings regularly.

Since there were sixteen people accused and all of them were represented by lawyers, the atmosphere in the courtroom grew more threatening with each passing day. With the special public prosecutor being neutral, we had to fend for ourselves. We expected the lawyers, being professionals, to argue the cases on merit while defending their clients, instead of getting personal with us. But their attitude became extremely appalling and disturbing.

One afternoon, after the court hearing was over, I was accosted by one of the accused, the manager of Uphaar Cinema. He threatened me saying, 'You speak too much. If you do not stop talking, I will see to it myself . . . I will shut you up. You do not know what I can do to you. I don't worry about the consequences and I will make sure that you will never open your mouth again.' Considering the seriousness of the matter, I reported the incident to the Tilak Marg Police Station. The police recorded my statement, but to our disappointment they chose not to take any action, thereby emboldening the staff of the Ansals and their lawyers to harass me.

Security was never a concern for both of us even though we were aware that by taking on the Ansals and the state, we had taken a huge risk. Had we been concerned about our safety and security, we would never have taken up this legal battle. On numerous occasions the case was listed for hearing in the Patiala House Courts as well as the High Court. I continued attending the trial in the Patiala House Courts even though I had to be alone there for hours on end, while Shekhar attended the hearing in the High Court. Shekhar was confident that I could take care of myself.

When parents think of their children fending for themselves, they can often get cowed by the thought. But after losing our children, we had nothing further to lose or fear. We had no great desire to live either. Hence, we continued our routine without any concern for our safety. We always carry photographs of our children in our wallets and the screensaver on our mobile phones is also a photo of our children. Whenever we needed strength, we just looked at their photo. It is their strength and determination which motivates us to continue fighting this battle.

The judge conducting the trial observed the attitude of the accused and their lawyers. To avoid any confrontation, the judge directed us to wait in the courtroom for half an hour after the accused and their lawyers left the court. We did as directed.

Since the trial was not progressing quickly, AVUT moved an application in the Delhi High Court to expedite

Unnati and Ujjwal

The Krishnamoorthys with their children

Unnati hugs Shekhar as she wears a saree for the first time for her school farewell

Cars damaged by the fire in the parking
lot at the ground-floor level

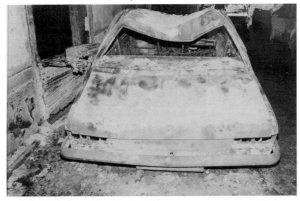

The Contessa car that first caught fire, setting the parking lot ablaze

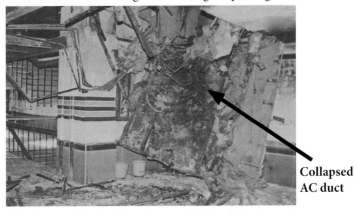

**Collapsed
AC duct**

The air-conditioning duct that caught fire and collapsed

Blackened pillar

The extent of damage caused by the fire can be gauged by the condition of the ceiling on the ground floor and the blackened iron pillars

The balcony and rear stall

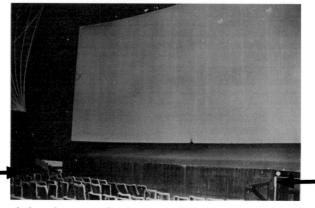

Exit

Exit

The exits below the screen for the rear stall that enabled patrons to escape

Bodies were removed from here

The toilet outside the balcony lobby from where some bodies were removed

Entry/Exit to box

The entry to the eight-seater private box

The private eight-seater box built for the family

The glass door leading to the staircase on the right-hand side was broken by the patrons

The lobby outside the balcony

Balcony entrance

Entry to the balcony from the lobby

The bolted door

The door from the lobby leading towards the staircase on the left was bolted

Private box

The seating arrangement on the right-hand side of the balcony had no gangway. An eight-seater private box was also erected in lieu of an exit

Six extra seats were placed right in front of the upper exit door on the left side, thus obstructing free access to the door

The extra seat on the left side of the balcony, which obstructed the escape route

No battery in the exit sign

There was no battery backup for the exit light

Broom instead of fire extinguisher

The fire safety management system in the hall—a broom was placed where the fire extinguisher should have stood

No microphone

The public address system in the hall — the microphone was missing

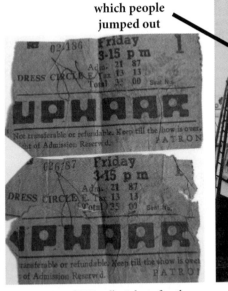

Windows from which people jumped out

Unnati and Ujjwal's tickets for the fatal screening of *Border* in Uphaar Cinema on 13 June 1997

Many patrons jumped out of the windows to save themselves

Members of the Association of Victims of Uphaar Fire Tragedy (AVUT) built a memorial, 'Smriti Upavan', in the memory of their loved ones. It is situated in an MCD park outside the burnt cinema hall. AVUT has been active in taking the case forward—holding havans and protests, apart from fighting the case in court

Photographs of the victims on a wall

The families of the victims have held several
havans in the memory of their loved ones

Candlelight march for the victims

UPHAAR CINEMA

BALCONY SEATING PLAN AS ON 13.06.1997

TOTAL NO. OF SEATS : 302

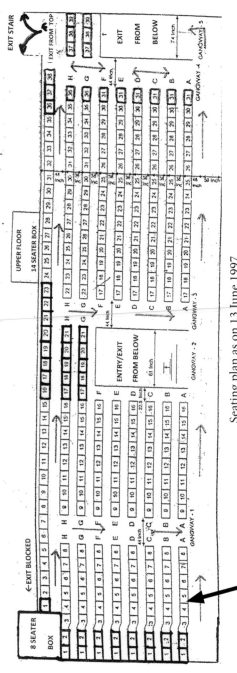

Seating plan as on 13 June 1997

Seats A4 & 5 where Unnati and Ujjwal were sitting on that ill-fated day

the framing of the charges. On 31 July 2000, the High Court directed the trial court to frame the charges 'or otherwise' by 16 October; otherwise in this context means that if there is no prima facie evidence, the accused could be discharged. Since the matter was being monitored by the High Court, it came up for hearing on 16 January 2001. When the hearing commenced, we were amazed to hear the judges declare that they were in receipt of a threatening letter. The presiding judge said that 'they cannot browbeat the court by trying to write such a letter. They have threatened the court by saying that you transfer the case within two weeks. I am constrained to see against whom I should take contempt of court action for writing such a letter. This court cannot be cowed down. Nothing can be achieved in my court by such a threatening letter even if they approach the Chief Justice of India.' (*Times of India*, *The Hindu*, 18 January 2001) The charges were framed by the trial court on 27 February 2001 against all sixteen accused charge sheeted by the CBI.

The order framing charges was challenged by all the accused in the Delhi High Court. Thereafter, four revisions came up before two different judges. All our efforts were directed to ensure that the trial was not stalled. To ensure proper representation in the High Court, we requested the CBI to engage the then solicitor general, Harish N. Salve, to represent us and our request was accepted. This came as a huge relief as it was important to be well represented to match the acumen of the leading criminal lawyers representing the Ansals.

Subsequently, the revision petition filed by the two MCD officials was dismissed on 28 August 2001, and the revision filed by Sushil Ansal and a manager of Uphaar Cinema was dismissed by the High Court on 11 September 2001. Gopal Ansal withdrew his petition and, with the passage of time, the other revision petitions became infructuous (ineffective and unproductive). AVUT had also filed a revision petition in the High Court for charging the Ansals under section 304 (II), because there was overwhelming evidence against them—showing that they had ample knowledge about the structural deviations in the hall and their acts of omission and commission were extremely dangerous and posed a substantial threat to the lives of the patrons. However, our petition was dismissed.

By now, we were well aware of the procedures and the working of the courts and hence, we decided against approaching the Supreme Court to challenge the High Court order. It would have, we reasoned, only resulted in delaying the trial further.

The trial court commenced with the recording of the statements of the prosecution witnesses. As witnesses, we were not allowed inside the courtroom while the statements were being recorded. We requested that the CBI expedite the recording of our statements, thereby enabling us to be present in the court while other witnesses deposed. Since it was the prerogative of the CBI to decide which witness was to be examined, they decided to drop Shekhar as a witness and only my statement was recorded. As a witness, I was harassed repeatedly by the defence lawyers on the pretext that they were not prepared to cross-examine me or due to their non-availability. I took a strong stand and conveyed to the judge that having already undergone major psychological and emotional trauma, it was unfair for me to prepare each time only to face the wrath of the defence counsels. I also requested the judge that my cross-examination be concluded on the next date of hearing.

I had expected the defence counsel to be sympathetic and treat me with dignity during the cross-examination, but

I was in for a rude shock. One of the counsels went as far as casting aspersions on my character, stating that he knows what kind of a woman I was. He went on to suggest that the tickets I had produced as evidence had been procured subsequent to my children's death and that I was misleading the court by saying that my children were sitting in row 'A' and their seat numbers were four and five. I was also questioned about whether my children were dead or alive when we found them, whether they were on the stretcher or lying on the floor, whether there had been a doctor attending to them and, if at all, how many doctors there had been. Even though these questions were irrelevant to the case, I made sure I answered them all. At one point, I replied that after seeing my daughter's body, I fainted and did not remember anything more.

At this, the team of defence counsels started laughing.

Disgusted, I told them not to make a mockery of my children's death. I warned them, 'God forbid, if you were to ever lose your children, you would not be able to do what I am doing as a mother!' I broke down completely then. How could one carry on in the face of such insensitive and incorrigible behaviour?

The matter was adjourned since I could not continue.

However, I was more shaken than we could have imagined. I began to lose all hope. As I was on anti-depressants, this episode triggered a bout of depression and in absolute despair, I decided to end my life. I took an overdose of tranquilizers. When Shekhar realized that I was losing consciousness and was vomiting continuously, he grew alarmed. On checking the medicine box, he realized what I had done and without wasting time, he rushed me to the hospital. The doctors performed a gastric lavage on me.

I was stable by the morning and after I regained consciousness, I requested the doctors to discharge me. Shekhar was very upset and, two days later, he had a detailed discussion with me. He reminded me of the promise we had made to our children and that by ending my life, I would only make things easier for the Ansals, thus falling into their trap. It took me a few days to recover emotionally, but this incident only made me stronger and more determined. I decided to face the cross-examination with confidence. I promised myself I would not get emotional in the court.

The trivial questioning by the defence counsels continued, but I stood steadfast and immune to their behaviour.

I had promised my children justice.

15

Eyewitnesses

The following are excerpts from the accounts given by survivors and victims during the court proceedings. We have included these to give readers an idea of what actually happened in Uphaar Cinema Hall that fateful day, how intensely the people in the balcony had to struggle to save themselves and the many safety violations that made it impossible for all of them to survive.

a) **Kanwal Bhalla was accompanied by her husband, daughter and a friend.**
Soon after the intermission, when the movie resumed, she heard a loud noise like a bomb blast and thought it was part of the movie's soundtrack. But she could soon heard voices crying, 'Fire! Fire!' and when she looked downstairs from the balcony, she found the stalls of the hall were empty. After some time the movie stopped playing and thick black smoke engulfed the balcony. There was no electricity, no announcement made on the public address system and even the emergency lights

were not working. The smoke was stinging their eyes and they felt suffocated. The Bhalla family and their friend all held each other's hands. They covered their noses with a piece of cloth to avoid inhaling the smoke. There was chaos in the balcony and they heard people saying that both the doors of the balcony had been bolted. It was pitch-dark inside. The people inside were trying to scramble out and they began moving towards the common exit and entry gate. Her husband insisted on going ahead and finding the way out.

He never returned.

She became unconscious and fell down, and regained consciousness only at AIIMS.

She was informed the next day of her husband's death.

b) **Karan Kumar was accompanied by his father, sister and his father's friend—Kartar Malhotra and his wife Kusum.**

They arrived five minutes before the movie started and they were seated in the balcony. After the intermission, they noticed smoke entering the balcony through the air conditioning ducts and from various other points. People started shouting, '*Utho, yeh kya ho gaya?* (Get up, what has happened?)' Their eyes started burning because of the smoke. The movie continued playing, but the lights went off. There was no exit light, no alarm and nobody from the management to direct them. There was a lot of commotion and everybody was desperate to find a way out of the balcony. By this time the movie had also stopped playing in the hall. People were trying to push open the main door, but it was locked and this only led to further panic. The Kumar family and their friends got up and caught hold of each other's hands, making a human chain.

Karan Kumar was leading the human chain, holding Kusum Malhotra's hand, who was followed by Kartar Malhotra, his father Kushal Kumar and his sister Kanika. He was only holding Kusum's hand, hoping that everybody else had followed him. He managed to reach the staircase where a lot of people were running up shouting, '*Aag lag gayi hai*!' (There is a fire!) In the ensuing commotion, Kusum fell down. Although visibility was extremely low, he picked her up and tried to find his way out. He somehow managed to come out of the cinema hall with Kusum.

It was only then that he realized that his father, sister, and Kartar Malhotra were not with them. He tried to go back inside the hall, but could not enter because of the thick smoke billowing inside.

He broke the cordon and somehow managed to run inside. By then people had started bringing babies, children and other persons, the dead, out of the Uphaar Cinema building. He went to the second floor where he found two firemen and two other people, all holding torches. He took the torches from them and started looking for the missing members of his family. He entered the bathroom and found several bodies lying one on top of the other. He could not find the members of his family. He eventually rushed to AIIMS, where he was informed that his father, sister and Kartar Malhotra had been brought dead from Uphaar Cinema.

c) **Ajay Mehra's wife and son had gone to Uphaar Cinema Hall. He received a phone call from his wife from the balcony lobby.**

His wife Rekha called him on his mobile phone at around 5.19 p.m., sounding hysterical. She told him that there was a fire in the cinema hall and they had managed to break open the balcony door, and had made it to the lobby with great difficulty. She added that there was smoke and gas all around her and there was total darkness inside the building; nothing was visible. She also told him that she was suffocating and there was no way out. She mentioned that Vedant, their thirteen-year-old son, had collapsed and that they were all dying. Her last words were a desperate plea to save Vedant.

Ajay rushed to Uphaar to locate his family, but he found his wife and son's bodies at Safdarjung Hospital.

d) **Satpal lost his brother and two cousins to the fire.**

Satpal Singh went to Uphaar Cinema Hall after receiving a call from Ravi Dutt Sharma, who had accompanied his brother and cousins to watch the movie at Uphaar that day.

Ravi told him that there had been a fire in the theatre. He added that he had managed to escape from the hall, but Kartar, Brahmpal and Virender were still in the balcony. On hearing this, Satpal rushed to the theatre. On asking the police, he was informed that no one was in the hall and that everyone had been taken to AIIMS. He did not believe the police and found a way to enter the balcony from the parking lot. He kicked open the door of the balcony lobby only to find total darkness inside. He saw some children and ladies lying unconscious on the floor. When he went deeper inside the lobby, he saw Kartar and Brahmpal were lying on the floor and Virender was sitting, his head bent towards the floor, his hands were on the heads of his brothers. All of them were unconscious. They were declared dead when they reached the hospital.

e) **R.C. Sharma, deputy chief fire officer, Delhi Fire Services, was a part of the rescue operation on 13 June 1997.**

On reaching Uphaar at 5.45 p.m., there was a huge crowd around the cinema hall; many ladies and members of the public were crying. Smoke was still billowing out of the rear side of the hall and through the windows on the upper floor. He heard that people were still trapped in the balcony. He entered through the staircase near the lift, and went up to the first floor. He found there was no fire, but firemen were cooling down the area as it was quite hot. He went to the staircase on the other side and went up to the balcony. There, he found the place full of smoke. He tried opening the door of the balcony foyer, but could not push it open. He immediately summoned some other officials to assist him. They forced open the door and found many people lying there, most of them unconscious. They started the rescue operation pulling people out via the staircase and the windows. With the help of others, he managed to rescue three people from the foyer. They were taken down to the ground level and handed over to the PCR van, which was parked there to help take people to the hospital. The rescue operation continued and the last body removed from the balcony was that of a little girl who, according to him, was still alive. He carried her down the stairs and sent her to the hospital.

The sight in the foyer had disturbed him greatly as he had never seen anything like that before.

He had accompanied the deputy commissioner (south), Naresh Kumar, on 14 June 1997, to assist him in the inquiry. He noticed then that the underground water tank by the side of the hall had a wire mesh fence constructed around it and some crates of cold drinks were kept there, thus making it impossible to draw water. The fire was confined to the DVB transformer room and the parking lot in front of the transformer room. The cables in the parking area were burnt and charred. They had seen sprinklers in the basement, but these could not be operated as there was no water in the system. The public address system was in the projector room, connected to the plug, but the mic was in the rewinding room. Emergency light fixtures were available in the cinema hall, but the emergency light was not attached to the fixture.

In 2002, the main investigating officer of the CBI was repatriated to Delhi Police when the trial had just begun. We were apprehensive about how the trial would progress without him, since he was conversant with all the documents pertaining to the case. We consulted Tulsi and inquired if we could move an application in the High Court to retain the investigating officer till the end of the trial. He was of the opinion that we were very familiar with the facts of the case, and it would be appropriate for us to assist the prosecutor.

In the absence of the investigating officer, the entire trial was conducted with the help of a constable who was not even a part of the investigating team. Had we not followed the case on a day-to-day basis and assisted the prosecutor, we shudder to think what its status might have been. While we do not intend to complain about the quality of the investigation conducted by the CBI, we would like to highlight the importance of the investigating officer, as well as the loopholes in regular procedure, which might prove harmful to such a case. In many ways, the officer holds the key to a good and thorough investigation, and his follow-up, presence and active participation in the trial is of tantamount importance. To transfer such an officer at a crucial time of the trial or investigation is to abet, perhaps unintentionally, the miscarriage of justice.

Only twelve witnesses had been examined by March 2002. The defence counsels were not cooperating and often sought to delay the process under some pretext or the other. They also sought frequent adjournments in the case. This was contrary to the provisions of the law. Section 309 of the CrPC stipulates that in every inquiry or trial, the proceedings shall be held as expeditiously as possible and in particular, once the examination of witnesses has begun, the same shall be continued on a day-to-day basis, until all the witnesses in attendance have been examined.

It was then that AVUT decided to move the High Court to expedite the trial. This was undertaken on 4 April 2002. The High Court directed the trial court to take steps to complete the trial as far as practicable by 15 December 2002. It was only after the intervention of the High Court that the matter was taken up for ten days every month, from 2 p.m. onwards.

A general practice followed in the courts is to summon three to four prosecution witnesses and allow them to depose on the same day. After the evidence-in-chief by the prosecuting agency, it is for the defence counsel to cross-examine the witnesses. It was often observed that after the cross-examination by one or two defence counsels, the others would seek adjournments on the grounds that they were either not prepared or busy in another court. The defence counsels continued to browbeat the judge by not completing the cross-examination of the witnesses on the day they were summoned, thereby forcing the witnesses to be recalled. The witnesses were bound by the court and asked to appear on the next date of hearing. This was done merely to harass and demoralize the witnesses.

We often heard the witnesses complaining about having to come to court again and again. We noticed several instances where the witnesses were recalled for cross-examination, only for the defence counsel to declare that he had no questions. This was merely done to waste the court's precious time. In our case, there were sixteen accused who were represented by sixteen defence counsels, and since each of them had the right to cross-examine the witnesses, the delay was enormous to say the least.

This attitude of the defence and the court granting them so much time in the form of adjournments immensely frustrated us. This was being done despite the High Court directions to conclude the trial by 15 December 2002. We were both worried that the witnesses being recalled repeatedly would discourage and dissuade them from deposing in court and would result in them turning hostile. Since we could not participate in the ongoing trial, we requested the public prosecutor to ensure that witnesses once called should not be sent back without being cross-examined.

One particular day, while one of the witnesses was deposing, the public prosecutor asked him to exhibit certain documents before the court. This was vehemently opposed by the defence counsels and the document was marked while the witness completed his deposition. We asked the public prosecutor to explain the difference between an exhibit and a marked document. He told us there was not much difference and the terms were used only to identify certain documents. We saw the same thing being repeated the next day and we realized that since the defence was objecting to the documents being exhibited, marking them had to be beneficial to them in some way. Why else would they object so vehemently? So we asked Tulsi to explain the relevance of an exhibit. He told us that a document exhibited in the court has to be original. The exhibited document can be appreciated as evidence, whereas a marked document does not have much evidentiary value. However, if a judge wishes, he/she can draw an inference from marked documents as well. He added that a witness can only exhibit the documents or case property if he is the author of the document or has witnessed the author writing the document in his presence and is familiar with the writing. A case property, on the other hand, can be exhibited if the person has seized the property himself or has been witness to the seizure. Only then, we realized the importance of an exhibited document. We assisted the prosecuting agency and ensured that whenever a witness came to court to depose, we would make a list of documents which he had dealt with himself, at any given point in time, or documents pertaining to his department. We also made a list of witnesses who had seized the document or case property during the time of investigation. This allowed us to ensure that most of the evidence was exhibited during the course of the trial and not marked, as desired by the defence.

We were glad that we were not mere spectators in the court, but managed to look through the strategies adopted by the defence counsels. We felt blessed that we had Tulsi to explain the legal technicalities to us.

16

A Brief Encounter

On 3 November 2002, there was a shoot-out at Ansal Plaza, an upmarket mall in the heart of south Delhi. This was also owned by the Ansals. The Delhi Police killed two alleged terrorists in the encounter. According to media reports, four days later a function was organized at Ansal Plaza to honour the special cell team. A cheque of Rs 1 lakh was presented to the joint commissioner, special cell, Delhi Police, as commendation by Sushil Ansal, the main accused in the Uphaar fire case.

Naturally, we were disturbed because the officer who received the cheque was the joint commissioner of Delhi Police (Special Cell) who had earlier served as DIG in the CBI and was in charge of the Uphaar case. The officer who had been associated with the case should under no circumstances have accepted favours from the accused, knowing that the prosecuting agencies have to stand by the charge sheet filed in court. This was a matter of concern because there were a number of prosecution witnesses from the Delhi Police who were yet to depose in court. In fact, the main investigating officer, who had been repatriated to the Delhi Police, was yet to be examined.

We decided to lodge a protest with the police commissioner of Delhi and visited the police headquarters on 11 November 2002. We were denied entry by the security at the gate who claimed that we could not take the car into the premises. I told Shekhar to park the car and join me inside. In the meantime, I went through the security check and while I was entering the headquarters, the officer who had permitted me access instructed two lady constables to stop me for reasons best known to him. On my refusal, they physically threw me out. However, there were some media persons at the venue. On seeing them, one of the officers called me and took the letter. The matter was widely reported in newspapers the next day.

Copies of the protest letter were also given to the Prime Minister's Office and the deputy prime minister. I received a call from the commissioner's office and was asked to meet him, at my convenience. I decided to meet him on 14 November and was surprised when I saw the security at the main gate; the man who had rebuked me the other day now walked me up to the commissioner's office. The commissioner expressed his sorrow at the behaviour of his staff on that day.

We confronted the commissioner about Sushil Ansal's reward and were informed that the police were under the impression that the function had been organized by the market association of Ansal Plaza and the cheque issued by the same. He denied that the officer who had accepted the reward on behalf of the special cell had been in charge of the CBI unit handling the Uphaar case. When I gave him the details about the officer's period of deputation from the Delhi Police to the CBI and his term in the specific unit, he relented. I demanded that the cheque be returned to Sushil Ansal. The commissioner, however, assured us that he would have it probed and if it was found to have been issued by Sushil Ansal or any of his companies, the cheque would be returned. It is ironic that the Ansals, who had earlier refused to pay a sum of Rs 1 lakh to the commissioners appointed by the High Court in our civil matter, readily produced the same amount and rewarded the police for the duty they had performed.

In January 2003, during the trial some very relevant documents went missing from judicial records, making conditions beneficial for Sushil and Gopal Ansal and an officer of the Delhi Fire Service who had given a no objection certificate to the cinema. The documents tampered with included a self cheque signed by Sushil Ansal for Rs 50 lakh in 1995 from the company that owned Uphaar Cinema, three cheques signed by Gopal Ansal between 1996 and 1997 from the company, the covering letter to the Minutes of the Managing Directors' conference, held with regard to Uphaar Cinema, chaired by Gopal Ansal in 1997 wherein he had directed the staff that 'not even a nail will be put in the cinema premises without his prior permission' and some relevant documents of the Delhi Fire Service. These were the documents that proved the financial and day-to-day involvement of the Ansal brothers in running Uphaar Cinema. Though it was an offence committed against the court, no FIR was lodged by the presiding judge. The loss, theft, mutilation or tampering of documents submitted in court constitutes a very serious offence, since it interferes with the administration of justice, and yet, no effort was made to seek permissible recourse. The CBI, being the prosecuting agency, should have moved an application for cancelling the bail of the accused, since one of the conditions imposed by the High Court while granting bail is that pending the trial, the accused shall not tamper with the prosecution evidence in any manner, directly or indirectly. But the CBI did not choose to do that. However, the court had permitted the CBI to lead secondary evidence, i.e., the photocopies of the original tampered documents, to proceed with the trial.

Ironically, around the same time, in another case that was unrelated to ours, relevant documents were tampered with, but the judge had lodged an FIR at once. It stands to reason, therefore, that one wonders why this was not done in our case as well. Once again, our intention is not to suggest any prejudice against us on the part of the learned judge, but to provide another example of the many loopholes that prevent the administration of justice. Time and again, the grapevine in the corridors of justice and investigation suggested that the investigating agencies, individuals and judicial staff are subject to pressure from different quarters. When pressure is exerted by powerful politicians, senior officers or bureaucrats, the chances of succumbing to the same become much greater.

Since the CBI did not take any action with regard to the tampered documents, AVUT moved an application to cancel the bail of the Ansal brothers and the officer of the Delhi Fire Service in the trial court on 14 February 2003. Our application was dismissed on 29 April 2003, on the grounds that the trial had reached the fag end and only the investigating officer remained to be examined. Aggrieved by the court order, AVUT filed a revision petition in the High Court on 30 May. In the meantime, an inquiry was conducted against the record keeper of the court by the additional sessions judge, who found him prima facie guilty of causing the documents to disappear, or to be mutilated or torn. On the basis of this report, the district judge terminated the services of the record keeper on 25 June 2004. After the dismissal, we moved the High Court for the registration of an FIR and an investigation into the matter. It seemed we were destined to discover every loophole in the justice system.

In the meantime the trial of our main case was progressing at a snail's pace, despite the High Court orders to expedite the trial.

Before the court proceedings begin, the names of all the accused are called out by the court staff to ensure their presence. In the initial years, the names of the Ansal brothers were called out in court, but with the passage of time, the Ansals' lawyers ensured that the court staff taking the attendance would skip their names. We presume that this was done because the Ansals wished to avoid the humiliation of being identified as the accused in an open court. These were some of the favours extended to the Ansals by the court staff.

We felt that the Ansal brothers were being given preferential treatment by the court staff because of their wealth; this courtesy was also extended to their family. In September 2003, the wives of Gopal and Deepak Ansal were summoned as prosecution witnesses to depose in court. During lunch hour, we noticed the Ansals present in court that day were allowed by the court staff to sit in the small library next to the courtroom. We had noticed the same thing on another occasion previously. This annoyed us and we reported the same to the presiding officer. We have been visiting the courts for almost two decades now, but such courtesy has never been extended to us.

Nevertheless, the examination of 115 prosecution witnesses was concluded on 7 August 2004. Fortunately for us, there were no hostile witnesses. Every witness stood by their statement and they were all consistent in their stand. The only eight witnesses who turned hostile were the ones we expected—namely, the Ansal family and their staff. Pranav Ansal's statement left us amused. Pranav was the director of Ansal Theatre and Clubotels (P) Ltd from 29 June 1996 to 28 March 1997, as per the records of the Registrar of Companies. While deposing in court, he stated that he had no idea if any financial powers were delegated to him and was not aware what the functions and duties of a company director were. He even claimed he was unaware whether Uphaar Cinema was being run by Ansal Theatres and Clubotels (P) Ltd to begin with. Either way, the Ansals' family and staff turning hostile had no ramifications on the case.

The next stage of the trial was the recording of the statement of the accused under section 313 of the CrPC. This began on 4 September 2004. The court had prepared around 879 questions to be put forth to the accused. The counsel for the Ansals argued that the court hand over all questions to them so that the lawyers could answer on behalf of their clients. Thankfully, this request was turned down.

In the beginning, as the accused's statements were being recorded, the media personnel were desperate to get a photograph of the Ansal brothers emerging from the court premises. They waited at different gates, but couldn't see the brothers enter the courtroom. They called us to ask if the Ansals were sitting in the courtroom, even though it was lunchtime. We decided to sit in the lobby and wait to see where and how the Ansals would enter the court. At around 2 p.m., we saw them emerging from the door connected to the lobby of the courtroom. The public was never allowed to use this door. On asking the court staff, we were told that the door was connected to a passage leading to the staircase that was marked as an exclusive entry/exit point for the judges. The Ansals had used this entry point to avoid media glare. We reported the matter to the presiding judge and the Ansals were restrained from using the stairs to enter the courtroom. It is ironic that being the owners of the cinema hall, they could not provide a safe exit to the paying public, but as the accused, they wanted a safe exit from the court premises.

Although the Ansals often enjoyed being featured on page three of various publications and newspapers, they hated their portrayal in the media as the accused. They came up with a canny way to avoid the cameras. They were always accompanied by their staff and security guards who carried umbrellas, irrespective of the weather. We soon realized that before the Ansals left the courtroom, their security guards would do a recce of the court premises to ensure that there were no cameras around. If they encountered one, the umbrella squad would come to their rescue.

During one of the routine hearings, I was alone in the Patiala House Courts as Shekhar was in the High Court. While Sushil Ansal's statement was being recorded under section 313 of the CrPC, an advocate filed her power of attorney on behalf of one of the managers of Uphaar Cinema. After lunch, when I was walking alone towards the court, I was accosted by the same lawyer and her colleagues. She told me in Hindi, *'Tu yahan par kya kar rahi hai . . . Tera yahan koi kaam nahin hai . . . Tu yahan se chali jaa nahi to tujhe yahan se maar kar baahar nikalva doongi . . . Tu shayad nahin janti, main* bar *ki* president *hoon!'* She asked me what I was doing in the court and then threatened that she would have me thrown out of the complex. She also claimed that she was the president of the bar and that I didn't know her powers. She was accompanied by twenty-five–thirty lawyers. It was evident from her behaviour that she had come to physically harm me. I was not deterred and told her firmly that Indian courts are open to all seekers of justice and that she had no authority to stop me, even if she was president of the bar. On hearing my reply she asked her colleagues to physically throw me out of the court premises. I lost my temper and told her firmly that they dare not touch me. In the meantime, a number of onlookers had gathered around us. On seeing this, the lawyers dispersed from the spot. Two reporters from a private news channel, whose identity I don't wish to reveal here, had captured the entire episode on their camera. They decided not to televise the footage. In fact, the reporters requested me not to name them in my complaint against the lawyer.

I brought the matter to the notice of the judge in charge of the Patiala House Courts. When I went back to the courtroom to attend the hearing, the same lawyer came into court and addressed the judge, pointing at me. 'Yeh iss court mein kya kar rahi hai? Iska court mein koi kaam nahin hai . . . yeh sirf ek gawah hai . . . aap isko yahan se baahar nikaliye.' She told the judge that I had no business being in the court since I was just a witness. She went on to add, 'Yeh court mein baadha daalti hai. Isko court mein se baahar nikalo. Mein bar ki president hoon aur yeh lawyers se misbehave karti hai. Mein isko Patiala House premises mein enter nahin karne doongi.' Her claim was that I interfered with the court proceedings and misbehaved with the lawyers, and that as the bar president she would make sure I couldn't enter the courts.

Thankfully, the judge intervened and said that I had never indulged in the activities alleged by her, and had never interfered in the proceedings of the court. At this point, the other defence counsels began to object to my being present

·off

in the court. One of the lawyers called me a bitch in Hindi and asked me to get out of the courtroom. The judge had to remind the lawyers that they were in a courtroom and not a college campus. The trial was stalled for nearly an hour.

This was apparently not enough for them. After threatening me, the advocate went to Gopal Ansal and told him, '*Aap yahi chaate the, na? Lo, aapka kaam ho gaya. Ab dekhna, agli date se court mein aane ki himmat nahi karegi. Agar aayegi to nateeja bhuktegi.* (You wanted this? See your work is done. Now watch; she will not dare to come to the courts in the next hearing. If she does, she will face the consequences.)' This was overheard by a member of AVUT, who was present in the courtroom.

The media was a witness to this altercation. The next day, the story was reported extensively by all the leading national dailies. We also gave a written complaint on 13 September 2004 to the judge in charge of the Patiala House Courts and a copy to the chief justice of Delhi High Court, the district judge, the presiding judge, the Bar Association of the Patiala House Courts and the Bar Council of Delhi. No action was taken against the lawyer.

We were pained to learn how the legal fraternity protects its own colleagues. Lawyers are expected to be the guardians of rule and law. They are the officers of the court and hence, cannot play its spoilers. It does not behove members of the bar to glorify themselves over hapless victims and litigants who are constrained to visit the court on the dates of hearing, hoping for justice.

Around the same time, an honest confession by a defence counsel for the Ansals left us amazed. He approached us and apologized for his uncivilized behaviour in court. He clarified that he had behaved in this manner because he felt compelled to please his clients. He openly admitted that had he faced a similar tragedy, he would neither have had the courage nor the tenacity to follow up on the case in the face of such a hostile atmosphere in the court. He further acknowledged that it was because of us that the trial was progressing. Otherwise, a case like this could never have reached any conclusion. On a lighter note, he told us that the defence counsels should be grateful to us instead of being hostile, because our persistence led to frequent hearings, due to which all of them benefited greatly and prospered.

17

The Accused

Sushil Ansal was the first accused to be questioned under section 313 of the CrPC. The first question put to him was, 'It is in evidence against you that on 13 June 1997, Ms Kanwaljeet Bhalla, along with her husband, friends Alka Arora and Payal, all went to see a movie at Uphaar Cinema from 3 p.m. to 6 p.m. and the ticket was for a seat in the balcony, which was purchased by Alka from the manager of Uphaar Cinema. What have you to say?' To this, he replied, 'I do not know as I was out of Delhi that day and I had resigned as director of Green Park Theatre Associated (P) Ltd in 1988 and, therefore, I had no connection with the working of the cinema or the company owning the cinema.' This answer amused us because a simple answer like 'I do not know' would have sufficed, since he is not supposed to know each and every patron who visits the cinema. But instead he went on to elaborate about how he had no role in running the cinema as though he was being questioned about his role in day-to-day affairs of the cinema hall.

His replies to the next six questions, all of which pertained to the same witness, were similar. During this time, we noticed one of his lawyers gesturing to him—that he had slipped up and had to be more specific in his replies. It was only then that he realized that the list of questions provided to him by his lawyers had probably changed as far as the sequence was concerned. We have no proof to substantiate this, but we did conclude that the prudent businessman was answering the questions in a very badly tutored manner.

Later, the counsel who had earlier shown a sympathetic approach towards us tried to mislead us by telling us that putting all 879 questions framed by the court under section 313 of the CrPC to each of the accused would be of no relevance and would have no bearing on the case. He gave us his unsolicited advice, saying that we should move an application in court stating that only relevant questions should be asked to each of the accused. According to him, the entire exercise was a waste of time and had resulted in merely prolonging the trial.

We were not convinced by what he had to say, and decided to study and understand the relevance of section 313. What we learnt was that this section is the fundamental principle that prescribes a procedural safeguard for the accused. It gives them an opportunity to explain the facts and circumstances that appear in the evidence against them. After reading some judgments on this section, it became clear to us that when important incriminating circumstances were not put to the accused during his examination under section 313, the prosecution could not place reliance on the piece of evidence, which could result in an acquittal.

In another attempt to prolong the trial, during the recording of Sushil Ansal's statement on 12 October 2004, his counsel raised objections to the questions put forth to him from the non-admissible documents that were marked, but not exhibited. An application was moved on his behalf, objecting to the admissibility of the documents. It was dismissed. The documents that had been marked earlier were now exhibited by the judicial order of the court on 23 December 2004. This order was challenged in the High Court by Sushil Ansal. On 1 March 2005, the High Court, while disposing of the petition, held that the accused would be free to raise a plea/objection in regard to the non-admissibility and non-proof of the documents, which would be decided by the trial court at the time of final adjudication.

Since the trial had almost reached its last leg, the atmosphere in the court had become very intimidating. The Ansals and their lawyers took every opportunity to frustrate us. During the hearing, the accused and their staff occupied all the chairs in the court and sat comfortably, reading magazines and texting. We had no choice but to stay standing for hours. As if this wasn't enough, the lawyers also objected to my leaning against a table. I pointed out to the court that being a victim, I was standing, while the accused sat comfortably. The judge saw the logic in my argument and directed all the accused to stand for the rest of the day.

However, this practice of the accused sitting in the courtroom during the hearing continued till the trial was concluded, because the Ansals' lawyers cited a Supreme Court judgment (Avtar Singh vs State of Madhya Pradesh) that allows the accused to sit during court proceedings in a prolonged trial.

As if this was not enough, throughout the trial, the Ansals received exemptions from appearing personally in the court. They were given special dispensation to attend to their businesses and to travel abroad for pleasure. Taking advantage of this, Sushil Ansal moved an application seeking permanent exemption from personal appearance to attend to his business engagements. He added that he could only devote fifteen days a month to his business and the other fifteen days were consumed by his obligation to appear before the court. The court dismissed his plea stating that he has been getting personal exemptions whenever it was required and the blanket exemption being sought on the grounds of business affairs cannot be granted.

In one instance, Sushil Ansal sought personal exemption to attend a dinner party hosted by the then chief minister of Uttar Pradesh in honour of former US President Bill Clinton. We wondered if Bill Clinton knew who he was dining with. Each delay, each unnecessary adjournment unjustly granted, corroded our belief that we would get justice for our children. But to see the person we wanted punished as a part of this official dinner angered us and made us lose faith in the system even more.

Though as victims we were not required to be present during the court hearings, we ensured we were present. But the accused found strange ways of getting personal exemption from the court proceedings. In one instance, an accused, who was an employee of the MCD, got exemption on medical grounds stating that he was suffering from severe diabetic neuropathy with weakness in both limbs, which calls for bed rest. But during the same period, the CBI found him performing as a singer in a devotional musical programme in the capital.

In another instance, a manager of Uphaar Cinema moved an application to attend the death anniversary functions of his father, while he was being examined under section 313. He got the matter adjourned. On inquiry, the CBI found that no such ceremony was being performed. Subsequently the agency moved an application seeking cancellation of personal exemptions, stating that the conduct of the accused made a mockery of the trial court and that they were misusing the concession to get exemption from personal appearances in court.

The statements of all the accused were recorded by 19 October 2005. By now, we had been fighting for justice for eight years. It was fixed that the defence's evidence would be recorded on 5 November 2005. An application was moved on behalf of Sushil Ansal to supply certified copies of the documents that would enable him to summon the defence witnesses. Their plea stated that they would produce defence evidence after going through the certified copies. This went on for over two months. The judge observed that the counsels for the accused were delaying proceedings, as copies of the documents had already been supplied to them. If they wanted to decide their defence, they could examine the documents in court, but this was not being done. The Ansals never produced any defence witnesses and it was apparent that this was just a ploy to delay and derail the trial.

By now we were well aware of the different game plans adopted by the defence counsels. Our patience was wearing thin, but there was very little we could do. It was for the prosecuting agency to take a strong stand and put an end to the delaying tactics. Fortunately for us, the court saw right through this strategy and pulled them up. But, despite this, it took nine months for the defence evidence to be concluded. Only three defence witnesses were examined by the DVB and DFS.

The defence evidence was finally closed on 2 August 2006. As per directions from the High Court, the judge visited Uphaar Cinema on 19 August to appreciate the evidence and a copy of the inspection report was supplied to all parties.

After the court hearing, we were walking towards our car when a gentleman called out to me. We stopped, realizing he wanted to speak to us. Though I could not recognize him, Shekhar immediately greeted him and told me that he was Unnati's accounts teacher. We spoke for about twenty minutes and we were amazed to learn that he remembered his first interaction with Unnati in 1996. He even remembered that after assessing Unnati for the first time, he was confident that she would get more than 90 per cent marks in accounts, failing which he told her he would refund her fees. He was proud that she had not let him down. We were touched when he told us that he still speaks about Unnati and her achievements to all his students.

The final arguments began on 26 September 2006 and Harish Salve, on behalf of the CBI, concluded his arguments in three days. Tulsi was not allowed to make an oral submission on behalf of AVUT, as it was vehemently opposed by the defence counsels, citing section 301 (II) of the CrPC. According to this section, only the public prosecutor or the assistant public prosecutor in charge of the case can conduct the prosecution. Our lawyer could only assist the public prosecutor and submit written arguments after the evidence was closed. Hence, we were left with no choice but to submit written arguments on 6 January 2007.

This was a setback for AVUT. We had a conference with Tulsi to understand how we could argue to bring the Ansals under the ambit of section 304 (II) of the IPC. He was of the opinion that the best way forward would be to file an application under section 216 of the CrPC, wherein any court may alter or add any charge any time before the judgment is pronounced. Hence, AVUT moved an application to convict the Ansals under a graver offence, i.e., section 304 (II) (culpable homicide not amounting to murder) as there was enough evidence against them. The application was disposed of on the grounds that the jurisdiction to entertain such an application directly from the third party did not rest with the court, since the application had not been moved through the special public prosecutor. If the court finds there is sufficient evidence, it will take a suo moto decision to frame an additional charge under section 304 (II).

The defence counsel commenced his arguments on 15 February 2007. The threats, intimidation and humiliation intensified, but we stayed focused on the case.

On 10 May 2007, after the court hearing, we were walking out of the courtroom along with other members from AVUT. We were discussing the day's proceedings when I noticed some of the Ansals' staff clicking my photograph on their mobile phones. The security accompanying them passed derogatory comments like '*Kutiya phir se aa gayi hai. Iske bachche to mar gaye hain lekin isko abhi tak chain nahin hai. Agar bachon ka itna khyal tha toh* Uphaar Cinema *akele kyun bheja*? *Kutiya apne aap ko* public prosecutor *samajhti hai. Pata nahin haramzadi kab maregi. Isne hamara jina haraam kiya hua hai.*' Meaning the bitch is here again. Even though my children were no longer alive I couldn't take their insults quietly. They also alleged that if I was so worried about my kids, why did I ever send them to Uphaar Cinema alone? They called me a bitch again and wondered when I would die since I had become such a nuisance in their lives.

I was disgusted to hear such insensitive and abusive language. I had never anticipated the staff of the Ansals would stoop so low. I decided not to respond since I had to maintain my dignity; instead, I decided to report the matter to the concerned judge.

I decided to submit a written complaint to the presiding judge, who, in turn, forwarded it to the additional chief metropolitan magistrate (ACMM), the administrative head. On the basis of my deposition and taking into consideration my earlier complaints, along with the deposition of other witnesses, the ACMM on 19 June 2007 took cognizance of the offence punishable under sections 188 (disobedience to order duly promulgated by public servant), 506 (criminal intimidation), 509 (word, gesture or act intended to insult the modesty of a woman), read with section 120 B (criminal conspiracy) of the IPC. The judge also summoned Sushil and Gopal Ansal, and their two employees. This was challenged in the High Court.

Meanwhile, in the main trial, the final arguments were being addressed by the defence counsels and the accused were seeking frequent adjournments. Frivolous applications were being filed by the accused for inspecting Uphaar Cinema, for clarification with regard to charges framed by the trial court and so on, all with the sole intention of delaying the proceedings. After the day's hearing, we both would leave the court frustrated with the attitude of the defence counsel. One day, we met some journalists who inquired about the day's proceedings. One of the reporters discreetly informed us that the defence counsel had no intention to conclude the trial and would keep delaying the process under some pretext or the other.

We were left with no option but to approach the High Court to expedite the trial once again. On 31 May 2007, the High Court directed the trial court to conclude the case by 31 August 2007 and recorded the court's displeasure that despite the previous order to conclude the trial by 15 December 2002, it was still proceeding at a snail's pace. The adjournments had been sought on behalf of the accused on several occasions and been granted by the learned judge merely on the counsel's request, contrary to the mandate of the court directing the additional sessions judge not to grant adjournments on the grounds of non-availability of the defence counsel. This means that an adjournment cannot be given simply on the grounds that the defence counsel is not able to attend a session. Various orders of the trial court show that adjournments were granted for this specific reason and other, similar reasons.

After the stern directions of the High Court, the matter was taken up every day from 10 a.m. to 4 p.m. As mentioned earlier, we were forced to stand throughout the day while the accused had the comfort of sitting in the courtroom. Long hours of standing without access to water or food took a toll on our health. Both of us developed painful back problems and I suffered from a spur on my heel. While we suffered exhaustion and bad health, the Ansals were being served soft drinks in the courtroom by their staff, even as the hearing was in progress. While such disparity in the treatment meted out to the victims and the accused is a tragic illustration of the power wielded by the wealthy, we would like to mention that since the arguments were in progress, it is possible that the judge may not have observed their behaviour. However, when I brought this fact to the notice of the presiding judge, remarking that it looked as though the Ansals were sitting in a board meeting rather than attending the court proceedings, the judge took a strong view and reprimanded them for their behaviour.

Their lawyers could not tolerate their clients being rebuked by the judge. They raised an objection and asked if the court was going to function as per the whims and fancies of the victims. They also challenged our presence in the court and our locus standi. I responded that the High

Court had passed the directions for day-to-day hearing
in a petition filed by AVUT. Since the High Court had
acknowledged our locus standi, how could they challenge it
now? The lawyers were dumbstruck and finally, continued
with their arguments.

This put an end to the boardroom culture in the court,
but we had to face the wrath of the lawyers till the end
of the trial. The arguments were finally concluded on
21 August 2007 and the judgment was reserved. By now,
four of the sixteen accused had already passed away due to
natural causes.

18

The Judgment

Ten and a half years after the tragedy, the trial court delivered its judgment on 20 November 2007, convicting all twelve accused as per the charges framed. The Ansals' counsels wanted the court to consider various factors: the nature of the offence, the role of the convicted, how the offence was committed, their age, background and those who were dependent on the convicted. We were dismayed when the counsel for Gopal Ansal put forward an emotional argument, stating that he was the only male member looking after his family—a wife and a daughter of marriageable age. Moreover, the counsel argued, he had deep roots in society.

This was especially shocking for us as during the course of the trial, the defence counsels had always maintained that the number of lives lost should not weigh on the mind of the judge and hence, the court should not get emotional. They had also submitted that prejudice and predictions should not surpass the judgment. Neither sentimentality nor anguish of any kind should enter the arena of the judgment.

The judgment was especially disappointing for us since the Ansals were awarded a mere two-year sentence. Someone accused of killing a chinkara (Indian gazelle) is sentenced to five years in prison, but those accused of having caused the deaths of fifty-nine innocent people could get away with just two years in prison, a pitiful twelve days in jail for each of the lives lost.

On the day of the sentencing, the courtroom was packed—there were members of AVUT, media persons, lawyers and the relatives of the accused. Once the sentence was pronounced, the spouses and relatives of the managers of the cinema hall started hurling abuse at us and threatened me. We were asked by the judge not to leave the courtroom. The situation was quickly spiralling into complete chaos and the police had to be summoned to control the crowd. The cops escorted us outside the courtroom, where a large number of media persons were waiting to record our reactions. I handed over an official complaint to the judge and the same was forwarded to the station house officer. However, as always, the police took no action.

Meanwhile, regarding the evidence that was tampered with, an FIR was lodged on the direction of the High Court. After a detailed investigation, a charge sheet was filed by the economic offence wing of the Delhi Police against the record keeper in February 2007. A supplementary charge sheet was filed against Sushil and Gopal Ansal, and four others in January 2008 under sections 109, 193, 201, 218, 409 and 120 B of the IPC. Subsequently charges were framed against all the accused by the chief metropolitan magistrate on 31 May 2014 under section 120 B (criminal conspiracy), 109 (abetment to crime), 201 (causing disappearance of evidence), 409 (criminal breach of trust by public servant) of the IPC. The order framing charges were challenged by the Ansals and the two other accused.

The judgment of the trial court convicting all twelve accused was challenged in the High Court of Delhi and the matter was taken up for hearing on a day-to-day basis. The senior counsel for the Ansals advanced their arguments, describing it as a case of the victims' anger and desire for revenge. While offering to give more compensation to the victims, he stated, 'We can provide them with soothing honey to heal their wounds. I do not know how much [money] my client has paid to them, if they want more we will provide them more.' His words suggested that our fight for justice was motivated merely by a desire to get money rather than a fair trial and punishment for the loss of innocent lives. He attacked us for speaking to the media frequently. 'The victims appear before the courts and media with bloodshot eyes and are thirsty for revenge. Anger and desire for revenge are futile. This would bias everybody's mind and persistent propaganda produces miscarriage of justice. After all, the judges are human beings.' We were not only offended by this belligerent and blatantly unfair statement, rather we were extremely shaken by the allegation. To our utter surprise, the presiding judge did not restrain the counsel. (*Times of India*, 29 February 2008)

We have noticed that the wealthy and powerful with the means to engage high-profile counsels do so not only to avail their legal skills and expertise, but also to take advantage of the many courtesies accorded them by the courts. By now, we can say with a fair degree of certainty that if a high-profile lawyer seeks adjournment citing even the most frivolous of reasons, he or she will be assured the adjournment will be granted without any fuss.

There were instructions that the matter be taken up on a day-to-day basis. It was listed thirty-seven times between January and September 2008, but was not heard for more than fifteen minutes on each occasion. During this period, the

Ansals were granted bail. Aggrieved by the bail order, AVUT moved the Supreme Court for cancellation, highlighting the conduct of the accused with regard to tampering with judicial records and intimidation. However, the CBI chose to move an application for cancellation of bail only for the managers. During the hearing of the special leave petition, the counsel for the CBI supported our plea for cancellation of bail for both Sushil and Gopal Ansal.

The Supreme Court issued bailable warrants against the Ansal brothers on 13 August 2008. It was Ujjwal's birthday and we had to be present in court that day. Since both the children's birthdays fall in August we like to stay at home on those days. The memories of all the birthdays we celebrated with the two of them brought us comfort and pain. But as the years went by, we were denied even this and we could not stay home as we were either attending court proceedings or having a conference with our lawyers. We sought comfort by constantly telling ourselves that the best tribute we could pay our children was by tirelessly seeking justice for them.

The Supreme Court observed that 'tampering with court records is worse than murder and dacoity . . . Whenever anyone attempts to tamper with court records, it is a serious offence and has to be dealt with sternly.' The court also observed that 'it was a blunder on the part of the trial court not to cancel the bail. The courts committed an error of law in not cancelling the bails.' While rejecting the argument of the defence that the documents from the trial court's judicial file could have been lost due to some negligence on the part of the court staff, the court observed that 'we are not English judges. We know what is happening in our country. It could be with your collusion too. After all, you were the beneficiaries . . . You are the kingpins . . . You are responsible.'

The Supreme Court cancelled the bail of the Ansals and their managers on 10 September 2008 on the grounds that the High Court ought not to have granted bail considering the circumstances of the case, especially in view of the conduct of the accused during the trial. The apex court further directed the High Court to fast-track the hearing by designating a bench exclusively dedicated to hearing the appeals on a day-to-day basis. (*Times of India*, *Hindustan Times*, *Telegraph*, 11 September 2008)

After the judgment, there was a sense of vindication and satisfaction among us. Our patience and perseverance had finally paid off and our belief in the judiciary was restored to some extent when both the brothers were incarcerated.

On 11 September 2008, the Ansals had to surrender at the Patiala House Courts by 3 p.m. We wanted to witness the surrender ourselves. But on reaching the court half an hour early, we were shocked to see the courtroom jam-packed. We thought that the Ansals had already surrendered. On making inquiries, we were told that they had still not arrived. In fact, the people in the courtroom were none other than their employees, who had come to show solidarity with their employers. We could sense the rage and anger they had towards us. It was with great difficulty that we managed to push our way to the front row of the courtroom.

Finally, when the Ansals arrived and surrendered, they were whisked away through a side door which used to remain locked all the time. Once again a safe exit was provided to the Ansals. The staff of the Ansals surrounded them to protect them from the media glare.

After the Supreme Court cancelled their bail, we attended a hearing of the criminal appeal in the High Court. The legal fraternity had mixed reactions to the judgment. Surprisingly, some lawyers congratulated us, even though they were not acquainted with us, while some were very critical of the judgment. It was around this time that a lawyer approached us and congratulated us for our achievement, and started talking about Ujjwal. We both looked at each other and wondered how this lady knew him. On seeing us looking perplexed, she explained that she was one of Ujjwal's teachers at Delhi Public School. She remembered him as a bespectacled boy, intelligent and mischievous, and also recalled that he was a good singer. What surprised us was that she used to be in the same school bus as him and was well aware of all the mischief he used to get up to. It made us proud that he was remembered so fondly by his teacher.

Time and again, people from different spheres of life have asked us how we have been so persistent in pursuing the path of justice for our children. At times, friends and family have cautioned us against letting the legal battle consume our lives completely. They remind us that perhaps we forget that even a victory in court will never bring back our children; so what is the purpose of pursuing these cases so intently?

At other times, lawyers and journalists asked us if we were being vindictive towards the Ansals in particular. They could not fathom how a group of ordinary people could stand against the powerful Ansals and refuse to back off even after a decade of prolonged legal battles. To all these questions we have a simple answer—if by pursuing the case relentlessly we can ensure that no other family in the future loses their loved ones to man-made disasters that are totally avoidable, our commitment to this legal battle and sacrifice will be duly rewarded. And if our persistence is perceived by some as us being vindictive, then so be it.

A review petition for bail was filed in the Supreme Court by Gopal Ansal, which was dismissed on 23 October 2008.

Subsequently, Sushil Ansal also filed a review petition on 15 January 2009, which was also dismissed.

It was the first time in ten years that the family members of the Ansals attended the court proceedings during the hearing of the appeal in the High Court. They were keen that the proceedings should not be prolonged and instead be concluded in the shortest possible time. They stayed in the court for the entire duration to ensure that their lawyers did not seek any adjournments.

The Ansals' incarceration had brought about a radical change in the attitude of their counsels too. The counsel for Sushil Ansal did not seek any adjournments and concluded his arguments within four days, displaying an alacrity that had never been witnessed by us during the trial. The rest of the accused also concluded their arguments within sixteen days, the CBI in four days and AVUT in two days. The entire appeal was concluded within twenty-six hearings.

The High Court pronounced its judgment on 19 December 2008, a year after the trial court judgment. The court upheld the conviction of Sushil and Gopal Ansal, the gatekeeper of the cinema, an officer from the DFS and two employees of DVB. However, the managers of the cinema, two MCD officials and one engineer of the DVB were all acquitted.

Though the court held the Ansal brothers responsible for all the deviations and violations in the cinema hall, the High Court reduced their sentence from two years to one year and a fine of Rs 5000. The sentence had been reduced taking into consideration that they were old, educated, had a good social status and no criminal background. If the law of the land is the same for everyone, irrespective of social status or education, why should the above factors be considered for the accused responsible for the deaths of innocent patrons?

The judgment of the High Court was challenged in the Supreme Court by AVUT, the CBI and the Ansals through different appeals and cross-appeals. The matter was to come up before the bench that had cancelled the bail. Three days before the scheduled hearing, the advocate on record for the Ansals wrote a letter to the registrar, seeking transfer of the cases listed before the bench. He expressed his reservations about the matter being placed before a bench, which comprised a judge about whom the senior counsel for Sushil Ansal had written a critical newspaper article. This was nothing but a bench hunting strategy, also known as forum shopping in legal terminology. If the lawyer felt embarrassed for some reason, the proper course of action was to recuse himself from the case rather than, in effect, asking the judge to do so. But the strategy was successful. The matter was listed in front of another bench. After spending four months and twenty days in jail, bail was granted to the Ansals on 30 January 2009.

After being granted bail, the Ansals stated that they had been targeted for no fault of their own and, in fact, they had suffered due to a misdirected campaign and were being punished for mistakes they had not committed. (*Times of India*, 24 January 2009 and NDTV, 9 April 2009)

Time and again, during the writing of this book, Shekhar and I have discussed and debated whether we should bare all and make public the names of the people involved in the various activities we have described here. However, we decided against it because we want to tell our story. But we must mention that it is only on the rarest of rare occasions in legal history that a counsel has approached the court to request the recusing of a judge. What is shocking is that the counsel who chose to do so was thus able not only to request the recusing of a judge, but also subsequently obtain bail for his clients. An ordinary citizen of the country, whether a victim or accused, could not have hired the services of such a counsel and would, under no circumstances, have the benefit of this power nexus, which can manipulate and deflect the arm of justice at will.

This was a clear case of criminal contempt of court and AVUT decided to file a proceeding against the senior counsel to this effect. As per the procedure, a criminal contempt can only be filed after receiving the consent of the attorney general of the country. The attorney general predictably declined to give his consent, stating that the court had recused itself from hearing the matter on the basis of the letter written by the advocate on record. He also stated that the court had not taken any suo moto cognizance in spite of the submission made on behalf of AVUT. Hence, the contempt petition could not be filed.

Predictably, the counsels for the accused were not available to argue the matter once bail had been granted, and they continued to seek adjournments between August 2010 and February 2012. The counsels' pattern became extremely clear to us—they were available for quick completion of arguments when their clients were behind bars, but did the vanishing trick once they were granted bail. Eight adjournments were sought by the counsel for Sushil Ansal in a span of two years between 2010 and 2012. In May 2011, an adjournment was sought on the grounds that the senior counsel appearing for Sushil Ansal, who was leading the matter, was unwell. However, as per media reports, he was arguing a high-profile case in the Patiala House Courts that day. (*Asian Tribune*, 6 May 2011)

We also noticed that once the matter is on board (listed for hearing), the court seldom accommodates the lawyers unless there are compelling reasons to do so. On one occasion, in another matter, the briefing counsel sought an adjournment due to the non-availability of his senior. The judges refused to accommodate his request and directed the briefing counsel to continue.

On another occasion, we heard the judges make an observation that senior lawyers were unavailable to argue since their clients were out on bail. But unfortunately, in our matter, the Ansals succeeded in delaying the appeal by two years, by seeking adjournments, and ultimately getting the benefit of the same.

During one of the hearings, the senior counsel for Sushil Ansal approached me and said that he wanted to speak to me after the hearing. I told him very politely that he could discuss whatever he wished to only in the presence of AVUT's lawyer. Typically, the defence counsel is not permitted to approach the victims and witnesses. Therefore, I was right in refusing to discuss anything with him, while he was in breach of protocol in this regard. Not surprisingly, my terse reaction left him disgruntled.

The arguments commenced on 16 February and the matter was to be taken up thrice a week. The senior counsel for Sushil Ansal carried on with his arguments until November 2012. One of the judges listening to the appeals went on to preside over another bench after the winter vacation and as a result, the hearing was stalled.

However, on 7 February 2013, the bench hearing our matter reassembled and passed an order stating that since the counsel for Sushil Ansal had argued the matter extensively over the last few months, all other parties were to be given time-bound periods to make their own cases. They made it clear that since the bench would be assembling especially to resume hearing of the appeals, the counsels should endeavour to stick to the time frame given to them.

The appeals came up for hearing on 5 March 2013. The arguments were concluded on 17 April 2013 and the judgment was reserved.

While reserving the judgment, the Supreme Court had issued a notice to the government of Delhi and the ministry of home affairs, Union of India. The court directed them to file a report on the steps taken by them with regard to the judgment delivered in the civil appeal on the Uphaar matter in October 2011, wherein the court had given suggestions to the government for consideration and implementation of safety measures in cinema halls.

The judgment was pronounced a year later, on 5 March 2014. By now, it had been seventeen years since the tragedy. While upholding the conviction of Sushil and Gopal Ansal, the court held that both were, at all material times, at the helm of the affairs of the company that owned Uphaar Cinema. All crucial decisions relating to the cinema, including those regarding the installation of a DVB transformer on the premises, closure of the exit and gangway, the rearrangement of the seating plan in the balcony had been taken by them. They had control over the day-to-day affairs of the venue until the date of the incident. They also had a high degree of financial control over the hall. Sushil Ansal was the representative licensee of the cinema hall. The complete shareholding of 5000 shares was with the Ansal family. The Ansal brothers had been occupiers of the cinema on the date of the incident and had the duty to care for the safety of its patrons. They had not been sensitive to the safety of the patrons and held it as a matter of low priority. They were more concerned with making extra money from the additional seats, rather than maintaining the required standards of safety. They were held grossly negligent for the death of a large number of people.

The Supreme Court findings were that the Ansals were more concerned with making a little more money out of the few additional seats that were added to the cinema in the balcony rather than maintaining the required standards of safety in discharge of the common law duty and also under the provisions of the DCR 1953. With such findings of the court, we have no hesitation in saying that the Ansals had violated all rules in order to satisfy their lust for money. Fifty-nine innocent people had to pay with their lives only because the Ansals wanted to make more money, eventually at the cost of ruining twenty-eight families.

The Supreme Court in its judgment further held that the seating plan was in contravention of the Cinematograph Rules. It also observed that after the cancellation of the 1976 notification, all the additional seats should have been removed. But instead the owners contested the same in the High Court. The High Court directed the Licensing Authority to allow only those seats which were in substantial compliance of the rules.

The court also held the authorities responsible for not insisting that the owners restore the exit on the right-hand side of the balcony, which was blocked by an eight-seater box. The judge further observed that the authorities, while applying the test of substantial compliance as directed by the High Court, had completely ignored important aspects like the presence of gangways and exits so vital for the speedy dispersal of patrons. The owners had asked to add fifteen more seats in 1980, compromising the safety of patrons further, which was allowed, thus taking the number of seats to 302. So many seats meant that there should have been four exits in the hall—this was another rule breach by the authorities and the Ansals.

The owners were aware that the hall was unsafe, given that there was a similar fire in 1989. Moreover, on several occasions, the violations had been pointed out to them by the authorities. The court also held that the Cinematograph Act imposes a penalty on the occupier of the cinema. Hence, the law does not treat the occupier as an ignorant person; rather the Act places an independent obligation upon the occupier to comply with the rules, irrespective of the assessment of the public authority.

The Supreme Court also rejected the owners' arguments that they blindly accepted the assessment of the Licensing Authority, stating that if such were the case, they should not have resisted the removal of the additional forty-three seats from the balcony. They should have ensured all the problem areas pointed out in the 1983 inspection were tackled and fixed.

The court also held that Sushil and Gopal Ansal owed the duty of care to the deceased persons, since they were in actual control of the premises and actively participated in the day-to-day management of the theatre.

While upholding the conviction, the judges disagreed with regard to the quantum of the sentence. Though the presiding judge upheld the sentence of one year awarded by the High Court, the presiding judge held that an equally important consideration that would weigh on any court is that of the prolonged trial the accused had faced and the delay of more than sixteen years in the conclusion of the proceedings against them. The judge further held that the High Court was justified in reducing the sentence to one year keeping in mind the delayed conclusion of the proceedings. Another circumstance which the court had considered was that the Ansals did not have any criminal background and were senior citizens.

In a rather contradictory fashion, the court cited the case of State of Madhya Pradesh vs Ghanshyam Singh (2003), 8

SCC 13, stating that the sentence must be proportionate to the offence committed and ought not to be reduced merely on account of long pendency, which simply means that the punishment given should have nothing to do with the time taken to arrive at a judgment.

We are told time and again that the scales of justice are balanced perfectly, tilting neither towards the accused nor the victims. Therefore, if the court decides that a prolonged trial demands a softer sentence for the accused, would it be unreasonable for victims like us to ask if a prolonged trial does not merit a harsher sentence for the accused, to provide some comfort to our grieving souls? Surely the court should take into consideration the number of frivolous adjournments sought not by us but by the accused, and then decide whether or not to give them the benefit of a prolonged trial. In the Uphaar case, it was the accused who sought needless adjournments and it was the accused who were given the benefit of prolonging the trial. The scales of justice in this case were not just tilted but bent towards the accused at the expense of the victims.

However, the second judge expressed the opinion that the High Court had indulged in misplaced sympathy by reducing the sentence to one year. The judge observed that the culpability of the Ansals clearly brought them under the ambit of section 304, as they were aware that such a tragedy was possible and the theatre had, in fact, witnessed a similar accident in 1989. The judge, while allowing the appeals of AVUT and the CBI for an increased sentence of two years, opined that this may be substituted with a substantial fine. The judge directed the Ansals to pay a fine of Rs 100 crore to build a trauma centre. The financial burden would be equally shared by the brothers, but in the same breath, the judge held that the sentence imposed on Sushil Ansal be reduced to the period already undergone, considering his age. The matter was referred to a three-judge bench, to be constituted by the chief justice of India.

The rationale offered for the reduction of the sentence was the prolonged trial that the accused had faced and the delay of more than sixteen years in the conclusion of proceedings against them. The court failed to appreciate that the delay was caused by the accused. Had the court examined the Trial Court Records, it would have become apparent that the accused were solely responsible for the delay. The delays were definitely intentional as they were well aware of the nuances of the criminal justice system. How could the court then have given them the benefit of the delay? In fact, it is the victims who, at every stage of the trial, approached the High Court for an expeditious trial in view of the frequent adjournments sought by the accused.

Though this judgment vindicated our stand the sentence awarded to the accused would not, we thought, have the desired deterrent effect. After appreciating such overwhelming evidence against them, the court had been very lenient towards the Ansals. In fact, we had expected the court to either order a de novo trial (retrial) or give them a maximum sentence of two years. Courts across the world allocate the burden of punishment to those who are capable of preventing such disasters. This is the only way to ensure that corporate conglomerates do not compromise on safety norms and selfishly endanger human lives.

But our hopes of setting such a precedent in India had diminished after seeing the final verdict delivered by the Supreme Court. For us it is nothing but a travesty of justice. What crime can be more heinous than the killing of innocent children to assuage economic greed?

In our country, the maximum punishment for a rash and negligent act is two years, irrespective of the number of people killed. This is nothing but a mockery of justice. In our case, the owners were convicted for death by negligence. A death is a death—either by negligence, knowledge or intention. No matter what the motive, the families of the victims are ruined.

Public spaces are governed by statutes that should be followed both in letter and spirit. Cinema halls are governed by the Cinematograph Rules which came into force in 1953 and were amended in 1983. The lawmakers could foresee that cinema halls, where more than 1000 people gather under one roof, should be subject to strict fire safety regulations. The wanton disregard of statutes should, we thought, be a case for charge sheeting the owners under the section for culpable homicide not amounting to murder. When the owners knowingly flout the rules and their acts lead to the loss of precious lives, the persons responsible should be convicted. If the prosecuting agency presses charges under more lenient sections, despite clinching evidence of the contravention of statutes, the courts should rectify the charges accordingly. We felt that the CBI should have charge sheeted the Ansals under section 304 (II) and not 304 A of the IPC, as the Delhi Police had done earlier. Was the CBI turning a blind eye to the clinching evidence against the Ansals with the sole purpose of shielding them?

This does not always happen when the perpetrators are less wealthy or powerful. In the Kumbakonam fire tragedy, for instance, which killed ninety children in July 2004, the Thanjavur trial court convicted all ten accused under section 304 (II) of the IPC. The accused were sentenced to ten years of rigorous imprisonment. The court had found the accused negligent for having provided inadequate exits, which impeded the escape of the children. Furthermore, the gates of the school were locked and the teachers abandoned the students. If the cause for both tragedies was so similar, then why was it that one court imposed a punishment of ten years to the guilty and a mere one year in the other?

Similarly, in the AMRI Hospital fire in Kolkata, which killed ninety people in December 2011, the accused were charged under section 304 (II) of the IPC by the sessions court in June 2016.

The verdict delivered in November 2014 in the South Korean ferry accident, wherein 292 people died, should be an eye-opener for our government and judiciary. The verdict came within six months of the date of the tragedy. While convicting the accused, the court awarded a sentence of thirty-six years to the captain of the ship, thirty years to the chief engineer and twenty years for other crew members for negligence, abandoning the passengers and overloading the ferry in order to make extra profits. They were given one week to appeal in a higher court. On 27 April 2015 the High Court reversed the lower court's verdict, accepting the prosecutor's argument that the captain, being seventy years old, had committed 'murder through wilful negligence' when he and his crew abandoned the ship and passengers, without taking the required steps to help them. The captain was sentenced to life imprisonment. The lower-ranking crew members received sentences of one and a half to twelve years in prison for shirking their duties in this regard. The court, while awarding the sentence, neither considered the age nor the social status of the accused.

In contrast, the Ansals were booked for mere negligence, though the acts in both cases are similar. In Uphaar, the patrons were abandoned and the number of seats increased in a bid to increase their profits. In the South Korean tragedy too the passengers were abandoned and the ferry was overloaded to make extra profit. Despite the similarities, the maximum sentence the Ansals can receive is a mere two years.

In the Republica Cromanon nightclub fire, in Buenos Aires in 2004, where 194 people lost their lives, the club operator was sentenced to twenty years imprisonment.

In the Lame Horse fire in Russia, in 2009, in which more than 150 people died, the executive director was sentenced to nine years in jail.

These comparisons prove beyond doubt that mass murderers are dealt with an iron hand in other countries. But the sentence awarded by our courts in the context of such disasters trivializes the gravity of the offence. Justice appears to be a mirage, a mockery or mere tokenism. Here, cases take decades to reach their logical conclusion. For instance, the Bhopal Gas tragedy in 1984, the Victoria Park tragedy in Meerut in 2006, and the AMRI hospital fire in 2011 are still pending in the sessions court.

While we were waiting for the three-judge bench to be constituted, Sushil Ansal moved an application in the court of the chief metropolitan magistrate, Patiala House Courts, Delhi, where he is facing trial for tampering with judicial records, seeking permission to travel abroad. We informed the judge that since he had been convicted, he should seek permission from the Supreme Court. However, permission was granted. We decided to move the Supreme Court to impose conditions and not allow the accused to leave the country without seeking the court's permission. The Supreme Court while hearing our petition expressed its displeasure over Sushil Ansal leaving the country without taking its permission. The court further stated that 'our grievance is they (Ansal and his lawyer) know that the matter is still pending and he did not take the apex court in confidence before leaving the country'. However, the court allowed Sushil Ansal to stay in the US after his counsel gave his word that Ansal would return to India on 11 April 2014.

This matter was listed in front of a larger bench, which directed the Ansals not to leave the country without its permission. Further, it was directed that the main appeal to decide the quantum of sentence should be listed for hearing after the summer vacation, i.e., in July 2014.

While the victims' families observed the seventeenth-year death anniversary of their loved ones on 13 June 2014, Gopal Ansal chose to move an application in the Supreme Court, seeking permission to travel abroad on the same date. The permission was declined, but the indifferent attitude of the Ansals towards the sentiments of the victims was exposed.

We waited patiently for the appeals to be listed for deciding the quantum of sentence as our matter was likely to be listed for 8 July 2014, as per the case status on the website of the Supreme Court. To our utter dismay, the matter was not listed for hearing and subsequently, the case status indicated that there were no further orders for listing. On making inquiries from the assistant registrar (listing), we were informed that the presiding judge who had passed the order had since retired. Specific orders were awaited from the chief justice. We moved an application for early hearing, but the registry of the court refused to entertain it, stating that our matter had been disposed of. We met the concerned assistant registrar and told him that this was contrary to the judgment passed by the division bench, wherein the court had directed the registry to place the papers before the chief justice to constitute an appropriate bench. It was also contrary to the status report of the Supreme Court website, wherein the matter was shown as pending. He said that the registry would make a decision after referring the matter to a senior. This approach outraged us. We brought this fact to the notice of the registrar (listing) and requested his intervention in the matter. Only after his intervention was our demand accepted.

Had we not been following up our case diligently, our matter would have probably never been listed, because as per the registry, our matter was disposed of. Since we were forced to make ourselves conversant with the working of the Supreme Court registry, we were not convinced by their explanation and approached the registrar to get the matter resolved.

AVUT's application was listed in the court of the chief justice on 8 October 2014, but it was dismissed with liberty to renew the prayer in a week's time. On 27 October, the matter was mentioned to the chief justice, but we were told that it could wait.

In contrast, when there was a dissent in the verdict by the division bench on 14 April 2015 in a matter relating to a powerful politician, a special three-judge bench was constituted on 22 April 2015 within a week. The said politician, who was convicted by the trial court and incarcerated, approached the concerned High Court for bail but the same was denied. The politician then approached the Supreme Court for bail and urged the court to grant an urgent hearing on bail plea. The matter was mentioned on 13 October 2014 and was directed to be listed on 17 October. The bail was granted without issuing notice to the state. This is when the politician had barely spent twenty-one days behind bars, while we as victims were denied an early hearing even though we had been waiting patiently for the last two decades. For our courts, the liberty of the accused is high priority whereas giving justice to the victims is of low priority.

19

Carrying On

In January 2015, AVUT and the CBI moved an application for an early hearing of the appeals. As we write this, we find ourselves smiling at the irony that we are calling this an 'early hearing', when, in fact, this matter has deliberately been dragged on for nearly two decades now. Nevertheless, our applications for the so-called early hearing came up in the court of the chief justice of India. A direction was given to list the appeals in April 2015. The verdict convicting the Ansals had come out on 5 March 2014 and the matter was finally listed for hearing on 21 April 2015. We were hoping that it would be taken up for final disposal and we would finally see the Ansals being sentenced. But once again, the Ansals' lawyer succeeded in delaying things by seeking an adjournment on the grounds that he was preoccupied. This resulted in another delay of four months.

The adjournment granted by the Supreme Court was a matter of great concern for us and we cannot help feeling betrayed by the system, at least to some extent. Before finally coming to the conclusion that the Ansals were guilty, our judicial system let the trial drag for almost sixteen years. No one seemed to spare a thought for the young people whose lives had ended so abruptly, for the victims or their families, whose lives were turned upside down by the tragedy. But when deciding on the quantum of sentence for the Ansals, the court suddenly felt sympathetic towards their old age and prolonged trial. A million angry questions crowded our minds. Who prolonged the trial for so many years? Who permitted adjournments for the most trivial and untruthful reasons? Who conveniently forgot that our beloved Ujjwal and Unnati were teenagers when their lives were snuffed out by the greed and dishonesty of two men, who knew exactly what they were doing when they flouted the laws?

Today, in a highly discussed case of rash driving and in response to public outrage, an offender who is technically a juvenile may now be tried as an adult, because it has been decided that he was aware of what he is doing. However, why did the judiciary turn a blind eye to the fact that the Ansals—as experienced, educated and senior businessmen—were very aware of what they were doing when they flouted laws? Why are we being treated differently? In the rash driving case, the juvenile/young adult in question may be charged under section 304 (II). But the Ansals were charged only with section 304 A, which is a rash and negligent act. Is this what our country calls justice? When is our judicial system going to become aware that the victims in our case have been treated so unjustly? Do we need to engineer media storms, candlelight vigils and other events to make the judiciary see reason?

The wait for justice seemed endless, but we laboured on because of our belief that we must establish accountability to avoid similar tragedies in the future. But this was not to be. Even though the matter was listed for hearing after thirteen months to decide the quantum of sentence by a three-judge bench, the Ansals succeeded in their mission to delay the matter further by seeking an adjournment. This move was arguably to take advantage of a prolonged trial and their old age at the time of final arguments on sentencing. Once again our hope for judicial closure was shattered.

In the midst of all this, there was another setback. The High Court, after eight years of granting an ex parte stay, decided the case with regard to criminal intimidation and insulting the modesty of a woman in July 2015. It exonerated Sushil Ansal and Gopal Ansal on the grounds that merely because they were employers of the other two accused, it could not be presumed that they had hatched a conspiracy with them to commit the offence. However, the court held that the staff of Ansals would face trial under section 509 IPC. Aggrieved by the order of the High Court, we filed a Special Leave Petition in the Supreme Court which was dismissed. Once again, the plight of the victim, in this case myself, was of no consequence.

The matter related to sentencing was listed once again on 4 August 2015 and, as expected, the Ansals' lawyer sought another adjournment and the same was granted. Fortunately, the matter was listed to be heard very soon after the adjournment, on 11 August 2015. This time, a senior counsel who had been appearing for the Ansals since 1997 appeared in court and sought an adjournment on the grounds that the earlier senior counsel had left the case. He misled the court claiming that he had been engaged only recently and hence, needed time for preparation. Adjournment was granted on these frivolous grounds and the matter was listed for 19 August 2015. It took seventeen months after their conviction for the matter to be heard, which in itself was unprecedented.

20

Freedom at Rs 60 Crore

The one lesson we learnt from all these years was that courts and their proceedings can be unpredictable. On days when we are able to retain our sense of humour, we often joke around and say that like a game of cricket in India, the results could go in any direction in the last minute. On other days, when we are despondent and tortured by the loss of our children, we feel immense anxiety and stress. On the night of 18 August we were restless and could not sleep; we kept wondering what the outcome of the two-decade-old legal battle would be. Would we be able to fulfil the promise we made to our children?

On 19 August we had to leave early as we had a conference with our lawyer. Before leaving the house, we lit a lamp in front of the children's photograph and prayed that they would finally get justice. We were optimistic that the Ansals would finally be incarcerated. Considering both our children were born in August, we hoped that the sentence would be a fitting tribute to them and the other victims of the tragedy. There was no ambiguity with regard to the conviction; the only question the larger bench had to decide on was with regard to the sentencing. On the way to the courts, we discussed among ourselves and came to the conclusion that in the worst scenario, the court would at least uphold the one-year sentence that had previously been granted.

Another reason for being optimistic was because, just a month ago, one of the judges who was now presiding over our matter was reported to have declared righteously, 'If a judge does not award appropriate punishment to a sinner, then he is equally guilty of breaching raj dharma.' He was referring to a case where he disagreed with another judge on the bench who was inclined to stay the execution of an accused.

The arguments began with the senior counsel for Sushil Ansal telling the court that he would take three to four days to conclude his arguments. He said he would try to persuade the court that the order of conviction was a wrong one. He argued that the owners of the theatre could not be held guilty for non-maintenance of the transformer by the DVB, which had led to the fire. He defended his right to seek a review of the verdict.

Hearing his plea, the bench said that they were not exercising review jurisdiction (the Supreme Court has the power to review any judgment or order made by it); their exercise was very narrow since it was a reference matter. But the counsel insisted that while hearing the reference, the court can go into the merit of conviction. He sought a lenient view in the matter saying that the world over, the basic principle was never to impose the maximum sentence. Tulsi countered this by saying that the counsel was raising stale arguments which had already been raised before and rejected by the court. He added that the victims wanted the Ansal brothers to be sent to jail and their sentence to be enhanced. To this, the bench said that in their view, the Ansals' conviction was confirmed.

During his arguments, the counsel for the Ansals stated that his clients were willing to pay Rs 20 crore each in lieu of a jail term. The court then asked the senior advocate, Harish Salve, representing the CBI and Tulsi whether they would be satisfied with this. Salve said that his instructions from the CBI were to press for custody. Our counsel also pressed for custody of the Ansal brothers.

The senior counsel appearing on behalf of Gopal Ansal did not hesitate to sing praises of the Ansals and said, 'We, like any human being, feel something terrible has happened. This is an opportunity for the court to allow them to do something for society. They have already done a great deal of work for the country. They are caught in an unfortunate situation.' We ask them, 'Is being responsible for the deaths of fifty-nine people an act of service to the country?'

The arguments continued after lunch and at around 3.30 p.m., the judges indicated to the counsel of the Ansals that he should conclude his arguments. Tulsi commenced his arguments at 3.40 p.m. The judges had some query regarding the trauma centre, which he addressed but he could not get an opportunity to make his arguments on sentencing.

Around 3.50 p.m., a few minutes after Tulsi started his arguments, the judges asked the CBI counsel to present their case. In a case of such far-reaching consequences, it surprised us that not even a counsel of Tulsi's stature and experience was allowed to argue for more than a few minutes. We should have understood that something was amiss. The CBI counsel requested that the matter be listed for the next day as Harish Salve was not present. However, the judges insisted that the briefing counsel argue the matter. It was pointed out that it would not be possible to present the facts of the case in ten minutes and the matter should be listed for the next day. This request was declined summarily and the counsel presented the matter orally without the benefit of any documents. Once again, such haste should have warned us that things were not going in our favour.

The briefing counsel appearing for the CBI said that it was not a question of compensation. The Ansals had been held guilty for gross negligence and blatant disregard of the law, leading to the deaths of fifty-nine people. An identical fire had broken out in the theatre in 1989 during a late-night show, but no corrective measures had been taken after that. They had flouted every law on the safety measures needed to run a theatre. Since they were educated businessmen, such negligence should be held against them. They should have realized the danger lurking in the theatre. They deserved to be made examples of in order to send a loud message to society.

The Supreme Court had repeatedly accepted the requests of the Ansals' counsel for adjournments on earlier occasions. But it refused to accommodate the CBI's request for a fifteen-minute argument on the next day. At 4 p.m., we were appalled when the judges pronounced the operative portion of the verdict, sentencing them to the period undergone (the time spent by the Ansals in prison) and a fine of Rs 60 crore. I was sitting in the second row and could not believe my ears.

It was as though the Supreme Court had pronounced that our children were not worthy of getting justice and that the Ansals, being moneyed, had the right to get away with killing fifty-nine people by merely paying a paltry sum of Rs 1 crore per person as blood money for a trauma centre. Are we to understand that all Indians do not enjoy equal rights as envisaged under our Constitution? Did these fifty-nine people not have the right to life? Does being moneyed and powerful empower the rich with some special rights that we are unaware of?

We realized that the lawyer had finally succeeded in his endeavour to convince the court that his clients should be allowed to walk free in lieu of money. This was our greatest fear and it had come true.

These two lines from the judge completely shattered our faith in the judiciary. I left the courtroom immediately to avoid an emotional outburst. I threw the files down and pushed aside whoever came in my way. I stood outside the Supreme Court of India, distraught and bereft of hope, tears streaming down my face as I spoke to the media. The Ansals walked past me with victorious smiles on their faces. I had just been robbed of my only hope of finding justice for the deaths of my children.

This judgment has ensured the message is heard loud and clear: only the rich and powerful are human, the rest of us are mere commodities with a price tag.

We came back home with heavy hearts that evening, wondering how we would face our children, in whose memory we light a lamp every evening; our house is still inhabited in a million ways with their memories. The children are gone, but we trudge through every day, living with only their memories. That is why we still talk of returning to our children.

On the way back home that evening, we were constantly on the phone giving the media our reactions. We entered the house very reluctantly and broke down after we lit the lamp; we were faced with the stark reality of the fact that we had failed to get justice for our children. As lots of television debates with regard to the verdict were lined up, we gathered the courage to participate in them. But we had no opportunity to speak to each other after the verdict. After the debates were done, however, we sat alone in the drawing room where the children's bodies had been laid on the ground on 13 June 1997. The day the final verdict was declared was, in many ways, as traumatic as the day of the tragedy itself. As parents, we had failed our children and despite our best efforts, we could not gather the courage to go into the children's room. Both of us sat up the whole night introspecting about where we had failed. We searched our memories desperately to see if there was anything that should have been done differently. Questions crowded our minds, but there were no answers. We wondered if the nineteen-year-long laborious legal battle had been worth it. We did not fight this battle because we wanted the Ansals to be poorer by Rs 60 crore. A sense of such immense failure overwhelmed us that we could not think of living another day. We wanted to give up then and there, both the legal battle and life. But we realized that we could not let this fight end so abruptly and in such a weak manner, since there were legal remedies still available to us. We decided then to go back to the court.

With a sense of shock, we also realized that the outrage we felt on hearing the verdict could well have pushed us off the brink. For nineteen years we had abided by the law and believed we would get justice for our children. The travesty that was passed off as a fair trial enraged us so much that we could have done anything that evening. We realized that the loopholes in the judicial system are such that they can turn even the most law-abiding citizens into criminals, capable of any act in a fit of rage and passion. That we were able to hold ourselves together that evening and not descend into committing a criminal act is a tribute to the immense love that parents have for their children and to the strength of the human spirit. If we found ourselves dragging our feet as we entered our home that evening, unable to face our children, would we have been able to face them had we committed an abominable act of violence in our rage and grief? But as we share these complex emotions and feelings with readers, we hope the judiciary will see where it leads countless unfortunate victims like us in its blind disposal of what it calls justice. They took us to the brink. We saved ourselves from falling off the brink, even when we were close to doing so.

The next day, the CBI counsel, Harish N. Salve, brought the matter up in court and requested that he be given time to address his arguments. He also mentioned that he had undertaken the case pro bono since 2000 and requested the court grant him fifteen minutes. If the court was not convinced by his arguments, they could throw the CBI out. The bench did not allow the plea and asked the CBI to file a review petition with all the points that had been left out in the hearing.

In its verbal order on 19 August 2015, the court had said that Sushil (aged seventy-five then) and Gopal Ansal (who was sixty-six) should pay a fine of Rs 30 crore each within three months. It had restricted their jail term to the period that they had already undergone in view of their advanced age. Modifying its order now, the Supreme Court restored the two-year rigorous jail term awarded by the trial court with the condition that the punishment could be reduced to the period already undergone if they paid the Rs 60 crore within three months. The court further held that if they failed to pay the amount within the stipulated time, they would have to undergo the sentence of two years each. The amount would be given to the chief secretary of the

Delhi government for setting up a new trauma centre or for upgrading the existing centres in hospitals managed by the government of Delhi.

A trauma centre in Delhi is by no means going to heal the trauma of the victims and survivors of the Uphaar tragedy. We have not come across any other case where the convicts have been asked to pay money towards the building of a trauma centre, which is the sole responsibility of the state. We did not give nineteen years of our lives to have a trauma centre built in Delhi with blood money. All we wanted was justice for Ujjwal and Unnati.

The court indulged the convicts by taking into account their age and the prolonged trial they faced. If the duration of the trial was to have any weight on the sentence, the court ought to have inquired as to who was responsible for it. The Ansals were responsible for the inordinate delays. It was AVUT that had repeatedly filed petitions before the High Court seeking an expeditious trial. We also realized that while granting the adjournments, the court often does not specify which of the parties sought them in the first place and on what grounds. There were also times when the court itself was perhaps not prepared or was preoccupied and, therefore, did not wish to hear the matter. Ambiguous statements about adjournments are then documented and, as a result, it becomes nearly impossible to keep an accurate and detailed account. If the judiciary intends to rectify and improve the existing system, making it possible for justice to be delivered speedily, it will need to take into account this glaring lapse. For those who wait endlessly for justice, like us, such delays and the lack of accurate documentation on adjournments remain the bane of our existence.

As we have reiterated before, the court let Sushil and Gopal Ansal off the hook because of their age. But the court's own ambivalent and watery consideration of age-related issues illustrates an unforgivable lack of fair and reasoned justice. In 1997, at ages fifty-six and forty-eight respectively, Sushil and Gopal Ansal had been responsible for the deaths of fifty-nine people. Yet, nineteen years into the epic legal battle, the same brothers were considered too old to be sent to jail. Their counsel, aged ninety-two, is not considered too old to argue their case before the court and bargain for their freedom. Is age to be manipulated and twisted at will in order to justify what can never be justified?

In recent times, some of the most high-profile and talked-about cases in the country have focused on the age of the accused. Therefore, it is important to mention that courts, instead of considering the age of the accused at the time of pronouncement of judgment, should consider the age of the accused when the crime was committed. In the case of juveniles, due importance is given to the delays in the justice system and they are given the benefit of being a juvenile at the time of committing the crime, thereby escaping a harsher punishment. To be more specific, the juvenile convicted of rape and murder in the Nirbhaya case walked free because he was a minor when he committed the crime. Then why should the age of the Ansals not be considered of tantamount importance while deciding the sentence? Why should they be allowed to walk free after paying a fine? The Ansals are not too old to play golf, travel abroad and conduct their day-to-day business. By this logic, Om Prakash Chautala, the former chief minister of Haryana, who is eighty years old (older than the Ansal brothers), need not have been sentenced to a jail term of ten years. Similarly, Sahara chief Subroto Roy, at sixty-seven, was sent to jail; how did the court think it was fair to send him to jail at that age then? After all, both Chautala and Roy are behind bars for economic offences and not for having killed anyone. On the other hand, the Ansals have been legally declared responsible for the deaths of fifty-nine innocent people, but have been permitted to pay for their freedom. This judgment has set a precedent wherein people above the age of sixty-five years will not be incarcerated, irrespective of the crime they have committed, provided they are rich and able to pay the hefty fine.

The Supreme Court, while giving a detailed judgment on 22 September 2015, said that the court was conscious of the fact that a matter of such magnitude called for a higher sentence, but it had to limit itself to the choices available under the law. However, the court reduced the sentence awarded to Gopal Ansal on the basis of parity with Sushil Ansal, whose sentence was reduced on account of old age. This could not be grounds for parity among the accused since the gatekeeper of the cinema hall was sentenced to two years imprisonment for the same offence. The inspector and the fitter of the Delhi Vidyut Board, who had repaired the faulty transformer, had been sentenced to two years imprisonment for a lesser offence under sections 337 and 338, read with section 36 of the Indian Penal Code. If the principles of parity were to be considered, there should have been more of it between all the accused. It is unjustifiable that just because Sushil and Gopal Ansal are rich and affluent members of society, their sentences have been substituted with a fine, whereas the other accused were handed a punishment of imprisonment.

This judgment has set a wrong precedent. If you are a wealthy and influential accused, you can drag the court proceedings on for decades and eventually, you might be able to buy your freedom by paying a hefty fine. The Uphaar judgment is an *uphaar* (a gift) to future affluent offenders. It will encourage lawyers to delay proceedings and, in the end, it will benefit their clients. As it is, there are enough gaps in our legal system that this precedent will be a legitimate one, as the judgment was delivered by a three-judge bench. This point was proved when one of the trial court lawyers asked us for a copy of the judgment to be cited in a case where his client was aged and he was arguing for a lenient sentence. This judgment has shown lawyers yet another way to make a mockery of our criminal justice system.

It is ironic that the Ansals did not even take two minutes to agree to pay the Rs 60 crore fine for their freedom. In contradiction to this, in 2003, in the civil matter, they had claimed that they had no money to pay compensation to the victims unless they were allowed to sell the cinema building. No money for victims but Rs 60 crore for their own freedom? It is pertinent to mention here that another accused from the Delhi Fire Service, who was awarded a sentence of one year, was asked to pay a fine of Rs 10 lakh. This approach of the court indicates that while awarding the fine, they considered the paying capacity of the accused. In comparison, the Supreme Court did not consider the paying capacity of the Ansals in the civil matter and reduced the compensation awarded to the victims by the High Court by almost half, holding them 85 per cent responsible for the incident.

Another aspect we wish to emphasize is that there is no precedent in India where a convict has been asked to pay a whopping sum of Rs 60 crore as a fine. By passing this judgment, a precedent has been set by the highest court of the land. This magnanimity was not shown towards the victims while awarding compensation. In the civil matter, our counsel was repeatedly asked by the judges to cite a judgment where an amount of more than Rs 10 lakh was awarded to victims. We wonder why the court could not set a precedent in the civil matter by enhancing the compensation. This would have helped the victims of similar tragedies in the future.

When two fishermen in Kerala were killed by Italian marines, their families withdrew the court case and had an out-of-court settlement that entitled them to Rs 1 crore each. On 30 April 2012, the Supreme Court expressed its extreme displeasure over the compromise struck between the families and the marines. The court termed the compromise 'illegal' and 'astonishing'. It further observed that the compromise defeated the Indian legal system and that Italy was playing with the process of law in the country. If this was the stand of the Supreme Court in this particular case, how did the Ansals walk free after paying Rs 60 crore as a fine to ensure the setting up of a trauma centre? Does this not defeat the Indian legal system too?

The judgment spawned several editorials penned by leading lawyers and senior journalists. The most intriguing article was written by Dr Rajeev Dhavan in Mail Online, with the headline 'Supreme Court has failed to give justice in the Uphaar case'. He had represented the Ansals in the civil writ petition. He began his article by stating that his reaction to the Uphaar case was unease and a huge burden of guilt. He accused the Ansals of having given false inducement to lawyers to stay with the case. According to him, after the High Court verdict in the civil matter, the Ansals met him along with another senior lawyer to solicit their advice. Both lawyers advised the Ansals to pay their share of Rs 12 crore as awarded by the court. The Ansals flatly refused to do this. The lawyers then asked that they pay Rs 8 crore or even half of that, but the Ansals turned this down too, stating that for a builder, Rs 12 crore could earn a profit many times over in record time. Aghast by their response, both the lawyers refused to take the case forward. Dr Dhawan termed the verdict of the Supreme Court flawed even if the age of the Ansals was taken into account, since the offences were not compoundable and there were no mitigating circumstances. He pointed out that delays had been caused by the Ansals' litigation tactics and justice had deserted the Supreme Court fully and totally. He concluded the article by saying that justice is only for the rich who can persist in strategy after strategy. The courts had shown indulgence to the Ansals, but society should never forgive them.

In another editorial in the *Deccan Chronicle* titled 'A Clockwork Justice', Anil Dharkar, a senior journalist, expressed his opinion that our judicial system upholds the traditional ideal of law—a woman in long robes, with the scales of justice in her hand, her eyes blindfolded so that she cannot differentiate between the rich and the poor, the powerful and the downtrodden. The Uphaar case is only the latest in a long line of cases which shows that the blindfold worn by our Lady of Justice is made of very, very fine muslin.

Since the fine imposed by the Supreme Court had to be deposited with the Delhi government, we met the chief minister. We requested him not to accept this blood money. We also told him that it would send a dangerous message to thousands of government employees. We also informed him that the authorities and employees of various licensing agencies such as the DVB, MCD and DFS had been held responsible for the Uphaar fire along with the Ansals. We urged him not to accept this tainted reward since it would make it look as though the government was being rewarded for colluding with the Ansals. The chief minister told us that since it was the judgment of the highest court of the country, he would have to seek legal opinion before declining to accept the money.

After my outburst to the media, the senior counsel of the Ansals called me insane in an interview with an

English news channel. I retaliated by saying that the threats, intimidation and abuse by his clients for nineteen long years were responsible for my alleged insanity. I believe lawyers like him will, in time, face their own demons but my stand is that when he denounces me publicly for being insane, he must know that he reveals to the world his complete lack of sensitivity towards a victim's grief. Of what use, then, is such sanity? Insane or not, my grief and tragic loss have made me sensitive to the need of the hour, to fight for public safety and accountability, not just for my children who will never return to me, but for children in general.

Nineteen years ago, I lost faith in god. Now, I have lost faith in the Indian judiciary. I have always had the greatest respect for the courts, but I am compelled to say that I am devastated by the Supreme Court judgment, which has given the Ansals the luxury of buying their freedom for a paltry (at least to them) sum of Rs 60 crore. Had it been the lives of the children of politicians or judges that were lost, justice would have been served within a year. But the judiciary could not understand the plight of a mother who has stood for nineteen years before the courts, only to face immense disappointment. Nobody cares about ordinary people, but the rich and powerful get away.

I regret having pursued the Uphaar case so vigorously for nineteen years. I should have just shot those responsible for the deaths of my children and the fifty-seven others. I would have pleaded insanity, exactly what the Ansals' counsel accuses me of. By now, I would have finished serving my sentence as well.

We had fought relentlessly for all these years, despite the various strategies adopted by the defence counsels. Our stand had been vindicated on 5 March 2014 when the conviction was upheld by the Supreme Court. We had immense faith in the judiciary, despite the fact that the majority of people we met discouraged us by saying '*kuch nahi hoga*', that nothing will happen.

In the last nineteen years, we have never protested nor did we take to the roads to publicize our plight. A lot of our well-wishers would tell us to follow the example of other cases where a media campaign highlighted the important facts, following which justice had been delivered. Since we had immense faith in the judiciary, we never felt the need to protest as the courts had always come to our rescue. The Supreme Court judgment that allowed the Ansals to walk free after paying a paltry fine was a huge setback for us. There was public outrage on social media and a lot of legal luminaries criticized the judgment. This outrage prompted us to organize a protest for the first time in nineteen years, on 12 September 2015 at Jantar Mantar, New Delhi. The protest was attended by the members of AVUT, their family members and friends. People from different spheres of life also joined in and political parties came forward to show their support for the cause. We were amazed when strangers walked up to us and showered us with compassion and solidarity, saying that we had not failed and it was the judiciary that had failed us. Several questions were raised and addressed during the protest. Had any lessons been learnt? Has justice been served? How do we ensure that no more lives are lost because of pure greed and recklessness?

We sent a memorandum to the President, the prime minister and the chief minister of Delhi highlighting the following issues taken up during the protest.

1. Justice for the Uphaar victims.
2. The urgent need to bring in new legislation to deal with man-made disasters, as suggested by the Law Commission in a consultation paper dated 20 July 2012.

3. The need to set up fast-track courts to deal with man-made disasters, to prevent mental and physical agony to the families of victims, caused by the flourishing adjournment culture that allows cases to drag on for decades. Such adjournments not only delay justice but also deny justice to the victims as has been experienced in the Uphaar case, which has dragged on for nineteen years.

4. Permission for videography of court proceedings to ensure transparency and strengthen common citizens' faith in the legal system.

My sentiments were echoed in the Parliament on 22 December 2015 by Derek O'Brien during a debate on the Juvenile Justice Bill. 'Had it been my daughter, god forbid, what would I do?' he had asked. 'Would I have trusted the laws of the country and hired the best lawyers or taken out a gun and shot him? I would have taken out a gun and shot him. So it is an emotional matter.' Even the lawmakers have lost faith in our criminal justice system.

This judgment will further alienate ordinary citizens from the courts. People consider courts unfriendly and utterly devoid of any compassion or ability to provide justice. This is a dangerous and explosive situation for what is considered a civilized society. If it is not rectified, it will force people to take the law into their own hands and allow anarchy to reign supreme.

The Ansals promptly deposited their share of money on 9 November 2015 with the chief secretary of the Delhi government, ten days before the deadline set by the court. This time they didn't seem to face any shortage of funds nor was there any need to mortgage Uphaar Cinema for raising funds.

The Delhi government accepted this money deposited by the Ansals. We, at AVUT, were very disappointed that the chief minister accepted this blood money despite the fact that the leaders of his party assured AVUT members during a protest that they would not accept the same.

Demoralized and aggrieved by the judgment, we decided to file a review petition with a prayer for an oral hearing in open court in the Supreme Court. A review petition should be filed within thirty days of the date of the written judgment and the petition is circulated without verbal arguments to the same bench of judges that delivered the verdict, seeking a review. We were fortunate that the CBI also decided to file a review petition. The matter came up in the chambers of the judges on 6 January 2016, where the applications for hearing petitions in the open court were allowed.

Since the matter was not listed, AVUT mentioned this in the court of the chief justice on 17 March 2016. He assured the counsel appearing for AVUT that the review plea would be listed for hearing after the Holi vacation. When the matter was not listed, AVUT once again mentioned the matter on 19 April 2016. The court said it would consult the concerned judges of the bench and explore the possibility of listing and hearing the plea during the upcoming summer vacation. Unfortunately, no orders were passed for listing the matter.

Even today, we have not been able to accept how the Ansals have been allowed to walk away scot-free by the apex court. We often wonder what if a member of kin of the Ansals is killed in a road accident—would the killer also be freed after paying a paltry sum of Rs 1 crore in lieu of the crime? Would the courts show the same magnanimity towards the accused and would this verdict be acceptable to the Ansals? We are very sure that the answer to this is a vehement NO.

In the nineteen years since the tragedy, Shekhar and I have witnessed drastic changes in some aspects of our lives, while other situations and feelings remain virtually unchanged. The old adage of time being a great healer has not been applicable to our lives. We still grieve for Ujjwal and Unnati as intensely as we did the day we lost them to the Uphaar fire. We miss them sorely at every single step of our lives. Time has neither healed our grief nor lessened it in any way. Our lives are permanently scarred beyond repair and we have accepted this.

What has changed drastically is our perception of the judicial system in our great country. Nineteen years ago, we started our battle for justice with the conviction that our children and the other victims of the tragedy would get justice. Sadly, the system has done everything it could to erode our faith in it. And if there was any vestige of hope left in our hearts, the final blow was served to us just recently when we read a newspaper report on 17 June 2016 about a ninety-two-year-old bedridden man being refused exemption by the Supreme Court from the life term awarded to him for a murder committed in 1980. If the ninety-two-year-old, bedridden Putti is made to serve his sentence in jail, despite his old age and ill health, are we not justified in wondering what made the courts exempt the Ansal brothers whose jail sentence was much shorter and who are relatively younger than Putti? Did Putti's age and ill health not matter to the Supreme Court merely because he does not have the means to hire a battery of influential lawyers to represent him?

Putti's is not the only case that reminds us cruelly of how we have been discriminated against by the judiciary. In a recent judgment on 25 July 2016, seventy-five-year-old Sukh Ram was found guilty of forgery. He requested a reduction in his six-month jail sentence by the Supreme Court on the grounds of severe illness and old age, but the court did not find his age and failing health reason enough for reducing his sentence. If his age and illness could not convince the court that his sentence should be reduced, even though the crime he committed was an economic offence and not life-threatening for anyone in any way, what made the court decide that the Ansals were too old to serve the prison sentence?

We are forced to leave a lot unsaid, but we do know that for us justice has been delayed and denied in the Uphaar fire case. Yet, we battle on, hoping for a miracle that will restore our faith in the judiciary once again.

We wish to conclude this chapter with a remark made by US Supreme Court Justice Robert H. Jackson who in the Brown vs Allen case, 1953, wrote in the concurring opinion, 'There is no doubt that if there were a super-Supreme Court, a substantial proportion of our reversals of state courts would also be reversed. We are not final because we are infallible, but we are infallible only because we are final.'

21

My Day in Court

I always wanted an opportunity to address the Supreme Court in person to tell them how a mother feels when she is deprived of justice, despite having spent all of her youth running from one court to the next. But as mentioned earlier, in our judicial system, the victims have no right to represent themselves in court during the trial.

However, on one momentous occasion, I grabbed the opportunity to speak my mind during the Supreme Court hearing of the case. By this time, the Ansals had been convicted and found guilty under section 304 A of the IPC by the trial court, as well as the High Court. AVUT's appeal was to enhance the charge from 304 A to 304 (II) of the IPC, or to increase the sentence from one year of imprisonment to two. The CBI too appealed for maximum punishment under section 304 A of the IPC. The Ansals, of course, appealed for acquittal.

During the hearing of the appeals in the Supreme Court, AVUT and its members, including me, were accused by the Ansals of taking up the cause for justice for monetary gain, considering how wealthy they are. Throughout the hearing in the trial court, the High Court and the Supreme Court, they had taken the same stand. This insensitive and false claim by the Ansals has angered and frustrated me over the years. As a mother, I could not fathom how they could make such despicable statements in court. Perhaps they felt they could substitute their children with money, but for me, this was impossible. Being wealthy, they thought they could get away by paying us some money in exchange for justice. But we were not up for sale. I was further anguished by the fact that none of the judges ever restrained their senior counsels when they made such allegations and offers.

This case was not about getting a windfall or any gains. I had not been able to spend a single penny on 13 June 1997 to save my children. My fight, as I said earlier, was not against the Ansals, but the system at large. I did not want another mother to suffer the same trauma and loss that I had. What the Ansals did not comprehend was that they could not put a price on my children's lives. For me, my children were too precious and priceless. Any attempt to compromise with the accused would amount to undermining the dignity of the dead. The Ansals never apologized to us; neither did they show any remorse nor did they offer their condolences. In fact, they never offered the slightest admission that they were to blame for the deaths.

On 4 October 2012, I got the opportunity to address the Supreme Court during the hearing of the appeals. While our criminal appeal was in progress, the senior counsel of the Ansals addressed the court, submitting that they were prepared to perform many positive acts, but the victims were not cooperating. He claimed that they had apologized to us, which was a false statement. The senior counsel went on to state that they were prepared to set up a trauma centre and take up many other philanthropic activities, but AVUT was not responding to their offers and instead was showing them a negative attitude. I was appalled when the judge reacted positively to these falsehoods, and asked us whether the compensation package offered by the Ansals could be explored and given serious consideration. I wondered how the court could even momentarily consider the offer when the crime the accused had been convicted for was not a compoundable offence—that is, the offence is so grave that the accused cannot be permitted to go scot-free. I was waiting for an opportunity to vent my anger. Initially, I felt handicapped since Tulsi was not present in court for that hearing, but ultimately his absence gave me the much-awaited opportunity to address the court myself.

Taking advantage of Tulsi's absence, the counsel for the Ansals manipulated the matter by submitting to the court that his clients were prepared to do a lot for the victims, but the victims were not prepared to accept it. He stated once again that they had apologized and wanted to set up a trauma centre. Unable to control my emotions and anger, or remember judicial protocol, I interrupted him mid-sentence and sought permission to address the court.

I submitted to the court that the approach of the accused was not worthy of consideration. All I needed, I said, was justice for the victims of the tragedy. I told the court that I had been fighting for justice for sixteen years, and would continue to do so until the case reached its logical conclusion. The senior counsel, realizing I was wresting away the sympathy he had elicited from the bench earlier, submitted that I could trust his clients as they were human. I retorted by saying that I would give more money than even they could, if they brought back to life at least engage the best advocates to fight over a range of trivial issues, bribe the investigating agency, bribe witnesses, delay proceedings, exhaust the witnesses and drive them up the wall, and finally dictate a compensation package of their own making and then get off scot-free. It is necessary to know what kind of crime they are being acquitted for—not any kind of murder, but mass murder.

I also brought to the notice of the court that the senior advocate arguing for the Ansals had concluded his arguments in the High Court in four days because his clients had been incarcerated. However, he had been arguing the matter in this court since 16 February 2012. The appeal in the High Court was concluded in precisely twenty-six hearings, but here he had been arguing for months. My objective was to drive home the fact that once his clients were granted bail, his aim was to delay the proceedings as much as possible.

The judges wanted to know whether the offer made by the Ansals could be used to improve conditions in society. I promptly replied that my counsel would address this issue on the next date of hearing.

When I walked out of court, I felt a sense of peace. I had finally been given the opportunity to address the court myself. I did not have to wait for very long for Sushil Ansal's apology in court to be exposed through the statement given y his counsel to the *Hindustan Times*. In this, he stated at Sushil Ansal had gotten very emotional. He said what wanted to and therefore apologized for the incident. But , it was not his fault.

n the next hearing (9 October 2012), Tulsi told the that the system could not improve unless severe ment and damages were awarded to the accused. o said that in other countries, damages are awarded nsurate with the wealth of the company and this

five of those who had been so cruelly snatched away from us. The judges immediately went into a huddle for a few minutes after this.

One of the judges asked the senior counsel to explain if his clients were contrite even in the least. The counsel said his clients were apologetic for something they had not caused. He lied and said that his clients had apologized, offered condolences through newspapers, even set up a trauma centre and now wanted to give more compensation. The judge asked him whether he thought this a good case for plea bargaining (an agreement in a criminal case between the prosecutor and defendant, whereby the defendant agrees to plead guilty to a particular charge in return for some concession from the prosecutor).

The answer was in the negative and, once again, the counsel for the defence explained that his client was open to compensating the victims for their irreparable loss.

I was privy to all this and was quietly listening in with mounting anger and frustration. At this stage, Sushil Ansal moved forward and submitted, in what appeared to be a very contrived and artificial fashion, that he too has children, grandchildren and knows how painful it is to miss them even for a day. He claimed that he understood the sadness and agony of those who had lost their loved ones in the fire. Then he turned towards me and tendered a formal apology, which seemed utterly hypocritical, and said that he would like to come to my house and apologize to me. During all these theatrics, I refused to look at the murderer of my children. However, I told the court that he was expressing regret and apologizing for the first time in sixteen years, and was doing so only because he was afraid the Supreme Court, being the final court of appeal, would sentence him to serving a long term in jail.

One of the judges asked me if this apology could be considered a step in the right direction. I immediately said that this was just part of a show being put up by the Ansals. I submitted to the court that for the past sixteen years, the Ansals had done everything in their power to thwart justice and had managed to evade the due process of law. They had never once apologized to me or the others. On the contrary, they had tampered with court records, threatened me to stop pursuing the case and even hired counsels to intimidate me into submission. The security guards who accompanied the Ansals to court had passed lewd remarks and intimidated me on the court premises.

The remarks hurled at me were so unimaginably vicious and vulgar that it is impossible for me to repeat them now. They were meant to break my spirit. I also informed the court that while cross-examining me in an insulting manner, the defence had accused me of being irresponsible for having sent my children to watch the film alone. I submitted to the court that it was the Ansals who had been responsible for the tragedy, but they behaved with no sense of responsibility to the victims. Sushil Ansal's half-hearted apology was a ploy undertaken to win the sympathy of the court. Once again, the judges went into a huddle for about five minutes.

Finally, one of them asked me, 'What would you do if you were given the role of a judge in your own case and asked to decide what is to be done if they were found guilty?' To this I replied instantly, 'Exemplary punishment, because it is necessary that such a message be sent to the corporate sector. They think that they can violate the law by bribing people.' Then I narrated a string of fire tragedies that had taken place after Uphaar. I mentioned the AMRI Hospital fire tragedy in Kolkata and pointed out that there were at least ten similarities between it and the Uphaar

tragedy, even though the two were fourteen years apart. No lessons had been learnt from the Uphaar tragedy and it only showed that the corporate sector was least bothered about public safety norms in its pursuit of generating maximum profits. I submitted that several similar tragedies were just waiting to happen. I pointed out that in the case of the fire at the Station nightclub in Rhode Island, in 2001, in the USA, where there were 102 casualties, the owner of the club had offered individual, handwritten apologies to each of the bereaved family members. Within a year, he was tried and convicted to fifteen years in jail. I also stated that I had spent my youth fighting in the courts to get justice. Once again, my arguments sent the judges into a huddle.

One of the judges said that although there were stringent laws against murder and rape, these crimes were still rampant, suggesting that little could be done in the matter of deterrence. To this I submitted that these are crimes passion and they will always happen. But incidents Uphaar are preventable. They would cease once cor players realize that being sent to jail is a reality for the law and causing death through gross neglige would start complying with public safety require

If these corporate players could spend a tin of their profits in safeguarding the public, inste same to bribe public servants to facilitate the for furthering their profits, points of pub like malls, airports, cinema halls and so or places. I added that if the owners did r of public safety and compliance, who remove any lingering doubts in the said that it is sad that in our system except human lives, is rising. Th bribe public servants to violate

acted as a strong deterrent. Here, this message has not been adequately delivered.

The bench responded by saying, 'You will have a judgment. We will take the matter to its logical conclusion.' It added that the charges against the accused were not compoundable.

I was relieved to hear then that the Ansals' power would not let them get away with this crime.

22

The Offers and the Bargains

Late one night in July 2002, around 2 a.m., somebody rang our doorbell. Shekhar answered it and we found a young girl standing on our doorstep. She apologized for having rung our bell by mistake and then rushed inside our neighbour's house, just across from our door. When the door opened we spotted blood on the floor of their house. We followed her inside and realized that our neighbour's daughter seemed to have slashed her wrists, causing profuse bleeding. I applied a pressure bandage to her wrist, and Shekhar and I rushed her to the hospital nearby. She was attended to by a doctor and her life was saved.

The doctor told us that had we delayed bringing her in to the hospital, it might have proved fatal for her. After she regained consciousness, she informed me that her parents were out of station. We took down their number and told them that their daughter has been hospitalized due to food poisoning, since we did not want to alarm them with talk of self-harm. By the next morning, they were back in Delhi and were extremely grateful to us for having saved their daughter's life.

However, this sense of gratitude was overtaken by greed when, six years later, the mother came to our house with an offer of sorts, supposedly from the Ansals. We told her very candidly that if the Ansals wanted to do anything for the victims of the fire, they should tender a public apology and accept the responsibility for killing fifty-nine people. She was aghast on hearing that this was all we wanted and said that if this was the case, it should not be a problem. The next morning, she returned with a sullen face and informed us (predictably) that what we were asking for was an admission of guilt, which the Ansals were not willing to admit. She said we could ask for any amount of money, but not an apology. We told her very categorically that it had to either be an apology and admission of guilt or nothing at all.

We thought that was the end of this chapter. But, to our surprise, two years later the lady returned, this time with her husband, calling on us under the pretext of having coffee. Shekhar and I knew that she had come with a message from the Ansals. They informed us that the Ansal brothers wanted to build a trauma centre and would like both of us to be part of the board. We were very firm and told our neighbours that we had no wish to associate with the killers of our children. If they were so keen to build a trauma centre, they could dedicate it to their own parents. But, despite our repeated refusals to entertain similar offers, the lady kept looking for an opportunity to speak to us.

The persistence with which she was advocating for the Ansals made us suspicious. Since she ran an NGO, we decided to visit the website of her organization. We were shocked to note that Ansal Properties & Infrastructure Ltd was one of the companies funding this NGO. Annoyed by her persistence, we told her in no uncertain terms that we did not wish to interact with her in the future. Our anger was also directed against the insensitivity of the parents whose daughter's life we had saved. Instead of feeling grateful, she was disrespecting our children, whom she had known from when they were extremely young.

In another instance, in July 1997, we received a phone call. The caller identified himself as a sympathizer and said he wished to meet us. He said he was in possession of some important information that he wanted to share with us. At that point, we were looking for any clue that would bring us closer to the truth about Uphaar Cinema. We decided to meet him in our office.

The meeting started on a very polite note with him offering his condolences at our loss. He introduced himself, but on seeing his visiting card we were shocked to learn that he was an employee of the Ansals. We decided to play along, thinking he might be a disgruntled employee who had some important information for us. He spoke at length about the Ansals' empire and their philanthropic activities. We patiently waited for him to come to the point and finally asked him about the purpose of his visit. At this point, he revealed that he had come to warn us to not meddle with the Ansals or we would face serious consequences. He claimed they were aware of our day-to-day activities and movements. Enraged, we asked him to leave the office immediately with the message that we had lost our most prized possessions, and we were now fearless and would not be deterred by their threats.

Years later, the same man showed up at Smriti Upavan on 13 June, as the memorial service was in progress. Both of us were alarmed since we did not want any unpleasantness that day. There was a strong media presence on the occasion and hence, we decided to ignore him. However, after the service finished, he walked up to Shekhar and informed him that he was no longer employed by the Ansals. He broke down and said that god had punished him for his insensitive behaviour by taking away the life of his son less than a year after he got married. He apologized and asked for our forgiveness. Shekhar sympathized with him about the loss of his son and assured him that we did not hold any grudge against him.

Over the years, we have been approached by different people several times to settle the matter with the Ansals. Strangers, friends and the most unlikely people have been commissioned to approach us with a wide range of deals and offers, all aimed at ending the legal battle we have fought relentlessly. No surprise then that we live almost as recluses, always wary and suspicious of people who could, in the garb of befriending us, suddenly make an offer on behalf of the Ansals. At times, we have also had to be cautious and wary, because the offers often come with thinly veiled threats and dire warnings.

23

The Media and Uphaar

In India, the media is considered the fourth pillar of democracy. It plays the crucial role of a watchdog. It is also supposed to hold up a mirror to society. However, today the media impacts the flow of justice and only those cases that are supported by a sustained campaign see justice in the end. This is even more evident when the cases involve the rich and the powerful, those who are considered worthy of media attention.

In our fight for public safety and accountability, the media has been our staunch supporter, and members of AVUT found reassurance and strength in their presence. In the initial years, AVUT organized panel discussions, seminars, inter-school debates and blood donation camps on the thirteenth of each month to coincide with the date of the tragedy. This effort of AVUT was widely covered by the media since most discussions at these events were related to public safety, emergency healthcare, food safety, corruption and fire safety. Nineteen years later, the Uphaar tragedy still holds the attention of the media, which continues to cover this epic battle for justice; all in a bid to hold government agencies and individuals accountable for ensuring safety in public places.

The Ansals often accused AVUT of targeting them because they are so wealthy. Their contention is that the Uphaar tragedy had merely been an accident and was being hyped up by the media. But it is a matter of record that although the media has by and large been supportive of the efforts of AVUT, there has never been public outrage or a media campaign for the Uphaar victims, similar to those for Jessica Lal (shot dead in Delhi in 1999 by the son of a rich and powerful politician) or Ruchika Girhotra (a fourteen-year-old who committed suicide in 1990 after allegedly being molested by the then inspector general of police). While we do not for a moment begrudge the attention these cases have received, it is also a fact that there were no candlelight marches for the Uphaar victims. On the contrary, the Ansals hired public relations agencies to change the perception regarding their involvement in the case. This resulted in articles in some leading dailies, whose writers did not even bother to check the basic facts of the case. One of the Hindi dailies even went so far as to report that the Ansals had been acquitted and the case against them closed. They accused AVUT of hatching a conspiracy against the family and prolonging the legal battle for a decade. This was reported on 20 July 2007, when the trial court was still adjudicating the matter.

In another instance, there was an editorial in a leading national English daily, authored by a renowned Page 3 socialite, published soon after the bail of the Ansal brothers was cancelled by the Supreme Court on 10 September 2008. The author chose to be a spokesperson of the feudal order, according to which no rich man can do any wrong. He was upset because the rich and powerful were being held accountable by law. He felt threatened because they, as a class, consider themselves above the law. In his words, 'Justice is increasingly being seen as a tool to punish the rich . . .' In his quest to defend the Ansals, he questioned the Supreme Court, asking if the chief justice of India would be held responsible or sent to jail for a fire on the premises. (*Hindustan Times*, 6 October 2008)

Another senior journalist made a reference to the conviction of Suhsil Ansal while talking about the judgment of the trial court in the Bhopal gas tragedy. He stated that Sushil Ansal had been convicted despite being a former director of the company, implying that he was not responsible for the day-to-day running of Uphaar Cinema at the time of the tragedy. He further stated that the genuinely guilty party, the DVB, had gotten away with the trial of a junior engineer. We only wish that the concerned journalist had taken the trouble of going through both the trial court as well as the High Court judgment before giving his opinion. (*Pioneer*, 14 June 2010)

It is a well-known fact that the government and the judiciary is under pressure whenever there is a public outcry or a media campaign. If the media decides to take up a cause, those specific cases given priority by the courts and fast-track courts are set up. Even the government machinery has a knee-jerk reaction and sometimes, even amends the law, as they did in the Nirbhaya case.

In the last two decades, India has witnessed many man-made disasters like Uphaar, where hundreds of precious lives have been lost. Although the media has highlighted these tragedies, there has never been a sustained campaign with regard to public safety. Had there been such a campaign, the government might have woken up from its slumber and taken some positive steps to avert such disasters. As of now, it seems public safety remains a low priority for both the government and the media.

It came as a rude shock for AVUT members that after the Supreme Court convicted Sushil and Gopal Ansal on 5 March 2014, the media, especially some TV channels, did not find it necessary to highlight the landmark judgment that ensured a huge step towards safer public spaces. It was the first time that the issue of public safety had received due attention and importance from the judiciary. Internationally, this would not have been a historic verdict because other countries hold the lives of their citizens dear and such tragedies are met with severe punishment.

Perhaps it would be appropriate here to mention the dramatic changes that the media itself has witnessed in the past two decades. In 1997, eminent journalist and news presenter S.P. Singh of Aaj Tak, known for his iconic sign-off, '*Ye thi khabrein aaj tak, intezaar keejiye somvaar tak*,' was reportedly in tears as he signed off on his report of the Uphaar fire. That was Singh's last bulletin and it is said that he wept for the agony and trauma of the families devastated by the fire. Indeed, we can only be grateful for such sensitivity and heartfelt support. In the decades that have passed, the media came under the control of corporate houses, and those who have the money to buy space and time in both print and electronic spaces. With corporate houses providing advertising worth crores of rupees, media houses are keen to please their patrons. Stories and reports can therefore be inserted or muffled, based on the price paid. Therefore, even if there are fearless, fair journalists around today, they could easily be silenced by the corporate bigwigs. And yet, despite these pressures, some journalists continue to support AVUT and report the case fearlessly.

24

Our Journey—From Parenthood to Advocacy

Advocacy was thrust upon us when we lost both our children. We have spent the last nineteen years grappling with the aftermath of a man-made disaster and now, as we write this book, we are ready to identify ourselves as social activists. Twenty-seven other families have been left with no alternative but to fight for justice, while those responsible for the deaths of our loved ones are free men. Briefly put, that is the story of how we became advocates for public safety.

You may well ask why we chose to fight this battle. The lives of AVUT members could never be the same after the tragedy. So, what are we fighting for? We are fighting to prove that those deaths could have been avoided. And if we, as a society, do not acknowledge the terrible greed and negligence that exists, and choose not to act against the gross violations of safety norms in public spaces, incidents like the Uphaar fire are bound to recur.

We were happy parents of two teenagers, Unnati and Ujjwal, until that cruel day when they were snatched away from us. The only thing our children did 'wrong' was that they had chosen to go to a theatre to watch a film. Our only mistake was to believe that no harm would come to them in a space that had been declared safe for its patrons. With our children gone, we felt like the living dead, condemned to fight for justice, and we identified ourselves as the 'victims'. This did not happen overnight. We lit funeral pyres. We cremated our loved ones. And as we did so, our only thought was: why our children? What was their fault? Why did fate have to play such a cruel trick on our family? We kept wandering aimlessly into our children's room, only to be hit anew with the dreadful finality of their eternal absence. We kept asking ourselves if we had failed them in any way. It had been our duty to protect them, but they were dead and we were alive. Why?

We decided that though we had not been able to save our children, we would not let those responsible for their deaths go unpunished. We wanted to ensure that people did not have to lose their lives merely because a cinema hall owner becomes greedy and decides to earn more profits. We did not want parents to grieve because some petty officials who were supposed to enforce rules, accepted bribes instead. AVUT was born out of terrible rage and endless grief.

After the judgment of the High Court in December 2009, upholding the conviction of the Ansals, it was evident that they would never be tried for a higher offence since they had been charged only with section 304 A of the IPC. We could not comprehend how man-made disasters could be treated merely as a rash and negligent act. While filing the charge sheet, the investigating agency should have realized that public spaces are governed by statutes, and the wanton disregard of the rules and by-laws should be brought under the ambit of culpable homicide. Thousands of innocent lives are lost in public spaces due to fires, but since our laws are so obsolete, the owners and occupiers do not think much of rectifying this.

Section 304 A of the IPC was introduced by the British as an amendment in 1870, meant to support British offenders and facilitate their escape in the name of the law despite committing serious crimes. Unfortunately, 146 years later, we are still following this law. The irony is that Britain now has strict laws to deal with man-made disasters. Further, punishment should always be proportionate to the gravity of the offence. Economic and social status or the advanced age of the accused or long pendency of the criminal trial, none of these can be construed as a factor for reducing the sentence.

Our endeavour, therefore, was to create a law to deal with man-made disasters so that the perpetrators of crimes of this nature are not spared in the future by merely invoking section 304 A of the IPC. On behalf of AVUT, we decided to submit a petition to the government to introduce legislation to deal with man-made disasters. Apart from the number of casualties being different, there is one common thread that runs through each of the mass tragedies that have rocked our nation in the last quarter century—all of them were man-made.

The Bhopal gas tragedy, 1984. Over 10,000 dead.

The Dabwali fire tragedy, 1995. Four hundred and fifty-two school-going children dead.

The Uphaar fire tragedy, 1997. Fifty-nine dead and more than 100 injured.

The fire in a mental asylum in Erwadi, 2001. Twenty-five dead.

The Kumbakonam school fire tragedy, 2004. Ninety children dead.

The Victoria Park fire in Meerut, 2006. Fifty-nine dead.

Kolkata's AMRI Hospital fire, 2011. Eighty-nine dead.

Kollam Puttingal temple fire in Kerala, 2016. One hundred and ten people dead.

Each disaster highlights the never-ending greed and/ or intentional ignorance of public safety laws. They also indicate that we have learnt nothing from these tragedies. Perhaps it is time to collate and analyse what happened to the perpetrators of such unpardonable crimes? How many of them were punished and to what extent? The answer is both shameful and disappointing as perpetrators are often booked under section 304 A of the Indian Penal Code.

This is a mockery of justice. The irony of the situation is that even the said provision is classified as 'bailable'— meaning that unless an accused is convicted, there is no fear of him being incarcerated, irrespective of the number of deaths he might have caused. Though it is popularly believed that criminal trials in our country take decades to conclude, in the unlikely event that an accused is unfortunate enough to be convicted for the said offence, he need not worry as he is bound to get relief from the appellate courts, because the maximum imprisonment provided is a mere two years. In this grim scenario, incidents of such catastrophic magnitude are bound to recur since there is no legal deterrence that can instil fear in the hearts of potential wrongdoers.

The need of the hour is to have appropriate legislation to tackle such man-made calamities, and an appropriate investigative and judicial mechanism that compels future offenders to think twice before indulging in acts of omission or commission that might endanger human life. The legislation must prescribe mandatory stipulations that need to be met by owners, occupiers and/or builders of places inhabited and/or visited by the public at large. Strict adherence to public safety norms and rules/regulations must be ensured through this legislation. Not only should adequate punishment be prescribed for the offenders, but care must also be taken that the punishment be of such a nature and degree that it has the necessary preventive effect. These cases should be fast-tracked and made time-bound.

We proposed to the executive committee of AVUT that we make a representation to the government to bring about a new law to deal with man-made disasters. Our suggestion was unanimously accepted.

A petition was drafted and we, along with other executive members, presented the petition for a proposed legislation to prevent man-made tragedies in public places to the then President, Pratibha Patil, the chairperson of the United Progressive Alliance, Sonia Gandhi, and the then law minister, Veerappa Moily. In 2009, the law ministry forwarded our petition to the Law Commission, directing it to come out with a law to deal with such disasters on a priority basis. We had several meetings with the chairman of the Law Commission and gave him many inputs, illustrating how such cases were dealt with in other countries. In 2012, the Law Commission published a consultation paper dealing with man-made disasters, which we are sure is collecting dust in an obscure corner of the ministry.

It is also pertinent to mention here that we received a copy of the letter from the additional secretary, ministry of law and justice, in July 2012 addressed to secretary, ministry of home affairs, recommending that they constitute the Fatal Incidents Claims Tribunal along the lines of the Motor Accident Claims Tribunal. This was in response to the letter written by AVUT referring to the Supreme Court's observation in its judgment on 13 October 2011 on the need for a comprehensive legislation dealing with torturous liability of state and its instrumentalities. But to our disappointment, all these recommendations and suggestions remain on paper and nothing concrete has been done about them, in spite of our honest and sincere endeavours in the past seven years.

With the change of regime at the Centre in 2014, we wrote to the Prime Minister's Office with regard to the legislation to deal with man-made disasters. We also sought an appointment with the law minister, but in vain. This makes us feel that the government is least interested in implementing this law, because today, it is the big corporate sector that owns various public spaces like multiplexes, hospitals, malls, etc., and the law we have put forth would make their heads directly responsible for all the deaths in case of any disaster. After all, power and wealth often have the upper hand in the battle between good and evil.

We were hopeful that since this law deals with public safety and the Law Commission had published a consultation paper on the subject, the government would take up the matter on a priority basis and would bring about a separate law to deal with man-made disasters. Despite hundreds of discussions in the media, nothing concrete has emerged till date. India is a country that reacts, but does not prevent. For our lawmakers, incidents like this are mere statistics. They are not aware of the names or ages of the victims who lost their lives and are not even aware of how many people are affected by a catastrophe. As an immediate response, the government announces financial relief. This is of limited help and is of no real value to the victims. More than financial assistance, victims need medical, social and emotional intervention. A one-time payment for a tragedy is by no means an effective answer. In fact, if the deceased is the breadwinner of a family, support for the education of the children and some sort of employment for at least one member of the affected family should be part of the package. To lose a family member is traumatic enough, but coping with life after a tragedy is the bigger problem.

Not receiving any response from the Centre, we decided to approach the Delhi government, since crime is a state subject. We met the chief minister, Arvind Kejriwal, on 21 August 2015 and apprised him of the need for a new law to deal with man-made disasters. He appreciated our concern and assured us that he would take up the issue in the Assembly, and bring about legislation to this effect at the earliest. But unfortunately, despite the assurance, nothing has been done till date.

Being victims of an unsafe fire culture in public spaces, we have long been advocating for change. It has always remained a matter of great concern to us that after 1997, we have witnessed a number of fire tragedies. We volunteered as citizen journalists for CNN-IBN, exposing unsafe buildings and forcing the Delhi Fire Services to take necessary action. We met the chief fire officer to learn the status of fire safety in high-rise buildings in Nehru Place, a well-known commercial centre in south Delhi. He claimed that Nehru Place was fire-safe. When we visited the site in 2007, we found a lot of faults in the buildings. There were no fire extinguishers, no fire buckets, no hose reels. Access to the terrace was limited, as the emergency staircase had been blocked with old furniture and boxes. Furthermore, the door to the terrace was locked. A year later, in 2008, we found that the situation had not improved. When we confronted the chief fire officer again, he was evasive. When the building was inspected by the CNN-IBN team later, the previous visits seemed to have had an impact and most fire safety measures were in place.

Exposing the problems in two or three buildings was not enough, as we were aware that there were many high-rise buildings flouting fire safety norms. We decided to approach the Central Information Commission. We moved an application stating that certain categories of essential documents, which chart the safety aspects of various buildings, should be published proactively on the website of the Delhi Fire Services under section 4 of the RTI Act, so that the general public is aware of the safety situation and omissions, if any. The commission agreed that this matter warranted larger public interest.

The commission discussed the matter with the chief fire officer. It was agreed that certain categories of information would be published on the department's website.

Losing a loved one is a very traumatic experience and more so when you know his/her life could have been easily saved. I met a bereaved mother who had lost her only child because he was not given medical emergency care in time after an accident. The child was taken to a private hospital and they refused to attend to him, citing that it was a medico-legal case. The child had to be rushed to a government hospital, but by then it was too late. This incident bothered us a lot. Incidentally, while we were doing some research for our own case, we came across a Supreme Court judgment that was of great interest to us. In Pt. Parmanand Katara vs Union Of India and Ors, 1989 AIR 2039, the court observed that 'Doctor is looked upon by common man as the only hope when a person is hanging between life and death, but they avoid their duty to help a person when he is facing death when they know that it is a medico–legal case . . . There can be no second opinion that preservation of human life is of paramount importance. That is so on account of the fact that once life is lost, the status quo ante cannot be restored as resurrection is beyond the capacity of man . . . No provisionally or fully registered medical practitioner shall wilfully commit an act of negligence that may deprive his patient or patients from necessary medical care . . .' This emphasized the need for making it obligatory for hospitals (government or private) and medical practitioners to provide emergency medical care to every injured citizen brought for treatment. The court also directed the Union and state governments and various High Courts to publicize this well.

We realized that though the judgment had been passed in 1989, no one was actually following it. This prompted us to move an application in the Central Information Commissioner, citing the Supreme Court judgment that display boards of appropriate dimensions be installed in private hospitals/nursing homes in both English and Hindi, declaring that it is obligatory for medical practitioners to provide emergency medical care in all cases of accidents and medico–legal cases under section 4 of the RTI Act.

The commission agreed with our take on the subject. By virtue of the powers vested in it under section 19(8)(a) of the RTI Act, 2005, it directed the department to fulfil its obligations and install the display boards.

Although we have won a few small battles, we are aware that much remains to be done in order to make public spaces safe. We continue to add relevant information, news, and media reports related to public safety on our blog, www.rememberuphaar.com. However, for public spaces to actually become safe for users, society will have to join hands with us to create greater awareness.

25

Lessons Learnt from the Uphaar Trial

Our involvement with the judicial system in India has given us some basic insights into the system that we feel compelled to share with readers. These are general observations, though they are rooted in the specific civil cases and criminal cases associated with the Uphaar fire tragedy.

To begin with, it must be understood that anyone who wishes to approach the judiciary to seek justice can do so only through certain filters installed in the system. Therefore, if you are the victim of a crime, you must first approach the police to file a complaint, and it is the police that investigates and decides which section of the IPC can be invoked. It is possible that at this initial stage itself, the investigating agency may be compromised or may soften its stand, especially if the opposing party is able to wield considerable influence. As a victim, you are helpless and can do little to ensure that your individual understanding is adequately reflected in the section of the IPC invoked in the case. The state becomes your representative, and decides which section of the IPC to invoke and which counsel should represent you in court. In our case, the state was unable to provide safety and the right to life for the fifty-nine people who lost their lives in the tragedy. But it was also the state, through one of its agencies that exercised the right to investigate the case, that decided which section of the IPC to invoke and selected a counsel that met with its approval. One cannot help but remember the powerful lines of Faiz Ahmad Faiz's priceless *nazm*, which reads:

> *Baney hain ahel-e-hawas muddai bhi, munsif bhi*
> *Kise wakil karen, kis-se munsifi chahen.*
> Facing those power-crazed that both prosecute and judge,
> to whom does one turn for protection, from whom
> does one expect justice? (Translation by Imteyaz Alam)

26

Legal Landmines

As litigants for the last two decades, we are fully conversant with the legal system and hence, are also aware of various landmines that obstruct the course of justice. Since landmines are used in war situations to trap, maim, kill and obstruct, it is important for the public to be aware of them and learn how to avoid them.

In an article titled 'India's Stagnant Courts Resist Reforms' in Bloomberg on 9 January 2015, the author speaks volumes about our justice delivery system. The article says, 'At the end of 2013, there were 31,367,915 open cases working their way through the system, from the lowest chambers to the Supreme Court. If the nation's judges attacked their backlog non-stop—with no breaks for eating or sleeping—and closed 100 cases every hour, it would take more than 35 years to catch up, according to *Bloomberg Businessweek* calculations. India had only 15.5 judges for every million people in 2013, then Prime Minister Manmohan Singh said at the time. The US has more than 100 judges for every million.'

It adds, 'The courts are plagued by *goondas* in black,' a phrase that pairs the Hindi word for goons with a sly reference to the black suit jacket lawyers wear in court. To keep collecting fees, these lawyers demand one hearing after another, with no intention of seeking a resolution for their clients, says Alok Prasanna Kumar, senior resident fellow at the Vidhi Centre for Legal Policy, which advocates for a more efficient system. Or, he says, they resort to extortion to make up for a lack of income. A 'significant number' of the lawyers, especially outside the capital, have practices that don't sustain them. That leads them to clog the system with pointless litigation. 'The bar in India is in a very bad shape,' Kumar says.

What started as a legal battle against the Ansals turned into a fight against the entire system. Apart from the Ansals and their employees, the other accused in the Uphaar case were staff of government departments. Section 197 of the CrPC requires sanction to prosecute a public servant, and therefore, sanction was required from the concerned departments for the officers to be brought to trial. It was as though they had sought permission from their departmental heads before indulging in unlawful acts. An officer who has breached the statute and gone beyond the scope of his official duties should not have the privilege of being protected by such a loophole. We lost close to five valuable months obtaining sanctions to prosecute the accused who fell under the purview of this section.

One of the most important factors that cause delays in any criminal justice system is the flourishing adjournment culture. We have counsels who specialize in seeking adjournments and who are referred to as adjournment counsels or adjournment specialists. There is an inexhaustible

list of excuses that an adjournment lawyer can successfully offer in court. Some of the most commonly used excuses are:
- the advocate is engaged in another court;
- the advocate has forgotten his/her brief;
- the advocate has personal difficulties.

We fail to understand the reason for the lack of professionalism that allows lawyers to cite personal difficulties as a reason for seeking an adjournment. Why do lawyers accept so many briefs when they know they can't commit fully to all of them? Every litigant looks forward to a hearing and spends a lot of time and money engaging a good lawyer. When adjournments are granted on the most flimsy of excuses, it is natural for the litigant to feel frustrated and disappointed. Who is to blame in these situations—the counsels or the courts?

A very interesting factor in our criminal justice system is that when the accused is incarcerated, the arguing lawyer is known to never seek an adjournment. If for any reason the court adjourns the matter, they plead for a very short date. Why is it not possible for our courts to see through this modus operandi? Once bail is granted, the defence counsels are unavailable and seek adjournments at the drop of a hat.

There is a specific section in the Code of Criminal Procedure which we are enumerating to educate a prospective litigant or a victim.

Section 309 (1) of the CrPC enjoins courts to conduct speedy trials and quickly dispose of cases. 'In every inquiry or trial, the proceedings shall be held as expeditiously as possible, and in particular, when the examination of witnesses has once begun, the same shall be continued from day to day until all the witnesses in attendance have been examined, unless the Court finds the adjournment of the same beyond the following day to be necessary for reasons to be recorded.

(a) no adjournment shall be granted at the request of a party, except where the circumstances are beyond the control of that party;

(b) the fact that the advocate of a party is engaged in another Court, shall not be a ground for adjournment.'

We have cited this section because during our ten years in the trial court, we have neither heard the defence counsels nor the public prosecutor refer to it while the trial was being conducted and all the adjournments were sought. Since the litigants are generally ignorant of the provisions of law, the defence counsels usually take advantage of it. We fail to understand why this section cannot be followed in letter and spirit as this would not only ensure speedy justice, but also bring down the pendency of cases.

During the course of the Uphaar criminal trial, adjournments were sought and granted on very trivial grounds such as:

- the accused cannot attend court after lunch because he is fasting due to solar eclipse;
- the lawyer forgot to get the file;
- the lawyer is not prepared to cross-examine the witness;
- the lawyer is busy in another court.

This has led us to the conclusion that adjournments can be sought for very random reasons and the courts will grant the same.

Courts should not grant more than three adjournments during the hearing of a trial and these should be granted only if adequate reasons are cited. The judges should be proactive and refuse to grant adjournments for the random reasons the lawyers cite. Another way of putting an end to this menace is that the courts impose heavy fines on the party seeking unnecessary and frequent adjournments, and the penalty thus imposed be given to the other side to offset their loss while engaging a lawyer. We are suggesting this because parties with a lot of financial resources usually resort to this kind of practice to frustrate the other party, and if the other party is a common man and cannot afford to pay lawyers indefinitely, the paucity of funds coupled with disillusionment and disappointment often result in the case being abandoned halfway through. This is the modus operandi of most rich and powerful litigants. Being officers of the court, the counsels should actually be assisting the court to expedite the proceedings, rather than seeking adjournments in the interest of their clients. All matters should be time-bound. This would discourage judges from granting adjournments. The only time when matters are expedited and no adjournments are granted is when there are specific directions from the superior courts.

In a recent judgment, Thana Singh vs Central Bureau of Narcotics, the Supreme Court held that, 'The lavishness with which adjournments are granted is not an ailment exclusive to narcotics (case) trials; courts at every level suffer from this predicament. The institutionalization of generous dispensation of adjournments is exploited to prolong trials for varied consideration.'

The court further held, 'Such a practice deserves complete abolishment . . . Often, the conclusion of examination alone, keeping aside cross-examination of witnesses, takes more than a day. Yet, they are not examined on consecutive days, but on different dates spread out over several months. This practice serves as a huge inconvenience to a witness since he is repeatedly required to incur the expenditure on travel and logistics for appearance in hearings over a significant period of time . . . Therefore, this court directs the concerned courts to adopt the method of "sessions trials" and assign block dates for examination of witnesses . . .'

Despite such strictures, adjournments are still lavishly granted.

Another factor which contributes to delays in legal proceedings is the superior courts' practice of granting a stay. What the courts do not realize is that it can prove to be detrimental in sensitive matters, especially those that concern public safety. The reason we are highlighting this is because in June 1983, after the Gopala Tower fire in Delhi, the lieutenant governor had ordered an inspection of all high-rise buildings in the city, including cinema halls. On 27 June 1983, the Licensing Department of the Delhi Police suspended the Uphaar Cinema licence for a period of four days and directed the licensee (the Ansals) to remove the alleged defects and objections during the period, failing which the cinema licence would be permanently revoked. Aggrieved by the order, the licensee filed a civil writ petition along with ten other cinemas in Delhi. On 28 June 1983, the High Court ordered the suspension order be stayed. This order was made absolute in June 1986, with further directions that 'if there is any fire hazards or no proper firefighting equipment, the respondent will be at liberty to call upon the petitioner to remove the fire hazard or to use proper adequate firefighting equipment and also called upon the petitioners to remove serious irregularities, if any, if the petitioner fails to comply with the same. The respondent will be at liberty to move the court or variation of stay order and for obtaining appropriate directions in this behalf.'

There was a serious fire at Uphaar Cinema on 6 July 1989, at 11.50 p.m., where both the transformers in the parking area on the ground floor caught fire and smoke entered the hall through the staircase and AC ducts. The smoke entered the balcony and other office areas. Fortunately, there were no casualties. Despite the directions of the High Court in June 1986, the Licensing Department neither informed the court of this incident nor did they make any efforts to get the stay order vacated.

The four-day stay order granted in June 1983 by the High Court continued till 13 June 1997. Had the court not granted this prolonged stay, the tragedy could have been averted. The courts should exercise restraint while granting a stay in matters related to public safety, since human lives are at stake. The stay is granted by the court to ensure that no injustice is done to the affected party. In the case of Uphaar, the owners had a blanket permit for fourteen long years to run the cinema despite various deviations and violations. It is ironic that the court revoked the licence of the cinema after the tragedy, by which time the action was too little and too late. The courts should be circumspect and ensure that no ex parte stay continues for more than a year. If the party which has obtained the same continues to seek adjournments, the matter should be dismissed at a heavy cost.

Another aspect that contributes heavily to the delays is the superior courts not deciding the revision petition filed against the trial court within the stipulated period of time. Whenever a revision petition is filed in the superior court, the trial court records are often called for and, as a result, the trial is stalled, even though there is no official stay order. The trial cannot proceed in the absence of the records. This process delays the trial proceedings. Hence, it is important for the superior courts to impose a time restraint and decide the matter quickly.

There should be fixed periods for the disposal of cases. Unfortunately, there is no time limit fixed either by an Act or a Code within which the cases must be decided. Hence, the counsels of wealthy and powerful litigants take it for granted that they can subvert the process of justice by unduly prolonging a trial. As a result, cases go on for decades.

We would like to share with readers some of the strategies adopted by the defence counsels solely to delay trials and get relief, if only temporary, for their clients. During the revision of one of our cases in the High Court, we were appalled when we overheard a lawyer in a case not related to ours telling his client that he was going to request the court to call for the trial court records, a move that he claimed would not be objected to by the other side since he had already spoken to them. Once the judge called for the records, he would ensure that the case was indefinitely delayed. We were very curious to learn how the lawyer would manage this and hence, we went to the courtroom even though the case being heard there was not of any concern to us. As he had predicted earlier, the lawyer managed to convince the court to summon the trial court records and received no objection whatsoever from the other side. Once he managed to get an order from the court, he asked his client to relax and celebrate, assuring him that the matter would be prolonged indefinitely.

Some readers may find this incredible and others might object to our showing the judicial system in such poor light. But anyone who wishes to prove us wrong only needs to examine countless other cases and will soon realize that such unsavoury practices are an accepted and known aspect of our judicial processes, which no one has seen fit to eradicate.

It does not matter how vigilant a litigant may be, the lawyers still have their ways of getting relief for their clients.

In order to obtain an ex parte stay in the superior court against an adverse order, lawyers are known to manipulate the registry into accepting an application filed by mentioning an incomplete name. This ensures that the complainant or other party is unaware of the matter being listed and thus, is denied the opportunity to oppose the stay order. To make it more clear, the method adopted is as follows. In one of our matters, the accused had filed a revision petition in the High Court against the summoning order of the additional chief metropolitan magistrate. The application was filed in the name of P.S. Sharma instead of Praveen Sharma. Similarly, the revision petition filed by Gopal Ansal was listed merely as Gopal. As the other party, this deprived us of the means to oppose the application since we had no way of knowing that P.S. Sharma and Gopal were none other than Praveen Sharma and Gopal Ansal. We have been victims of this strategy where the court granted an ex parte stay which continued for eight years. Although there are a lot of checks in the registry, some unscrupulous lawyers find ways to hoodwink the court and use the loopholes to their benefit.

One of the major drawbacks of a prolonged trial is that the witnesses are called to depose in court after decades and, with human memory being short, it becomes very difficult to remember and restate what they had purportedly stated during the investigation of the case. Criminal cases largely depend upon the testimony of witnesses. A witness who had given a statement before the police about the crime is required to repeat the statement years later in court without any key material modifications, failing which the statement is completely discarded. Since cases often come up for trial several years after investigation, the witnesses who had given a statement to the police have either passed away or cannot be traced since they have relocated to different areas. Their statements, regardless of how important they are, would not be considered in evidence against the accused facing trial.

A witness turning hostile is a common feature. In fact, there are instances where witnesses have deposed supporting the prosecution's case, but then turn hostile during the subsequent protracted cross-examination. Delay in the disposal of cases affords greater opportunity for the accused to win over the witnesses by intimidation or inducements. There is no law to protect the witnesses and they are often treated very shabbily.

Prolonged litigation undermines public confidence and weakens democracy and the rule of law. Early disposal of a criminal trial is also advantageous for the accused so that their innocence can be proven, rather than remaining enmeshed in a criminal trial for years on end, rendering them incapable of getting on with their lives and businesses.

In the case of Babu Singh and Ors vs the state of UP, Justice Krishna Iyer said, 'Our justice system, even in grave cases, suffers from slow-motion syndrome which is lethal to "fair trial", whatever the ultimate decision. Speedy justice is a component of social justice since the community, as a whole, is concerned in the criminal being condignly and finally punished within a reasonable time and the innocent being absolved from the inordinate ordeal of criminal proceedings.'

Civil suits in our country are lengthy, dilatory and expensive. It is not feasible for an ordinary Indian citizen to file a writ petition or civil suit to claim damages. We do not have the concept of lawyers working on a contingent basis with a conditional fee agreement. The usual form of this agreement states that the lawyer will accept a case based on the understanding that if lost, no fee will be charged.

We strongly believe that this kind of contract between the litigant and lawyers would be of immense help. To quote Walter Olson, a legal analyst based in the USA, 'There are things lawyers will do when a fortune for themselves is on the line that they won't do when it's just a fortune for a client.'

According to the law, a contingent fee is defined as a 'fee charged for a lawyer's services only if the lawsuit is successful or is favourably settled out of court. Contingent fees are usually calculated as a percentage of the client's net recovery.'

However, if the case is won, the lawyer will be entitled to a percentage of the damages awarded by the court. This makes it easier for an ordinary citizen to defend their civil rights since otherwise, to sue someone for a tort, one must first be wealthy enough to pursue such litigation in the first place.

A contingent fee also provides the lawyers with a powerful motivation to work diligently on the client's case and strongly oppose any adjournments sought by the opposite party to expedite proceedings. This will ensure speedy justice for the litigants. In other types of litigation, where clients pay the attorney per appearance, it makes little difference to the lawyer, whether the client eventually wins the case or not. Further, it is beneficial for the lawyers if the trial is prolonged.

The practice of a contingent fee system will be a boon to litigants from different strata of society. There are several cases where people have been wronged, but they do not take legal action in the fear that they will not be able to meet the lawyer's fee and other expenses. This will be a boon to them. Lawyers in the United States of America and the United Kingdom often take contingent fees.

The reason why we are in favour of lawyers working on a contingent basis is that there are very few public-spirited lawyers in this country who are willing to take up cases pro bono and ensure that the case reaches its logical conclusion, even if it takes decades. If lawyers are allowed to work on a contingent basis, many of them would come forward to take up cases for poor clients who have merit in their case. This kind of arrangement will ensure that justice is accessible to the poorest of the poor in this country.

However, there should be a safeguard to discourage false claims. If a frivolous claim is filed, then the cost borne by the affected party should be reimbursed by the claimant and his lawyer.

27

Voiceless Victims

Our experience of visiting courts for the last two decades in pursuit of justice has made us realize that the term 'victims' stands for those who are victimized, intimidated, condemned, traumatized, insulted, muted and stifled. Victims, who should be an integral and protected part of our criminal justice system, are actually the losers in this system. The present system shows far greater concern for the rights of the accused. It is heavily loaded in their favour, and victims are often termed the outsiders or remain totally neglected. Every crime has a victim and ignoring him/her challenges the very basis of human rights. An unfamiliar and hostile criminal justice system, providing no support mechanism and no witness protection programme, cumulatively deters the victims and makes justice inaccessible.

Victims are further at a disadvantage when they cannot participate in the day-to-day trial and are forced to be silent spectators. This means that according to the CrPC, we as victims cannot represent our case ourselves or through a lawyer engaged by us for the purpose. The code mandates that it is only the public prosecutor appointed by the state who can appear on behalf of the state, and the victims or their counsel can, at best, assist the prosecutor with his/her consent. While this state of affairs undoubtedly reflects the desire of the state to protect and represent the victims on one hand, it also exposes the gaping holes in the process, on the other. What this amounts to is that the accused have the right to be represented by a battery of reputed experts and legal luminaries, especially when the accused is both rich and powerful. The victims, on the other hand, must be satisfied with the state-appointed public prosecutor, who despite his/her best intentions, may be burdened with too much work to do the intensive study required for such complex cases. At any given point in time, a public prosecutor may be attending to more than fifteen to twenty matters listed in each court, making it virtually impossible for him to prepare himself to argue every matter extensively. Each case has separate facts and circumstances, for which a lot of research is necessary. The offices of the public prosecutors are not well equipped and do not have enough secretarial staff. Therefore, victims have no choice but to accept that they will be represented by someone they are not familiar with, whose abilities they are not certain of, who in turn may not be familiar with the complexities of the case and who invariably functions in the most difficult situations. In these circumstances, there should be an amendment to the Code of Criminal Procedure giving rights to the victims to participate in the trial in order to ensure that society does not lose faith in the judicial system. Victims of crime today feel left out and ignored. What the system needs is certainty, swiftness, severity and recognition of the rights of the victims.

Neither at the stage of framing the charges nor at the passing of an order of discharge are the views of the victim ascertained, let alone considered. The state does not find it necessary to consult them during the course of the trial. Let us for a moment examine this situation hypothetically, in order to reveal the many loopholes that have caused such a tragic erosion of our faith in the system.

When a crime is committed, a complaint is usually filed by the victims or a third-party complainant who may not be affected personally by the crime—for instance, a bystander who witnesses an accident. On the basis of that complaint, an FIR or first information report is lodged, after which an investigation is carried out by the investigating agency, such as the local police force, CBI or CID. The investigating agency then prepares a charge sheet based on the evidence collected against the accused and files it in the court, where the court takes cognizance of it. At no point in the investigation or the framing of charges do the victims of a crime have any say in the matter and the system too does not think it necessary to consult them. As a consequence, there is every possibility of the investigating agency or the public prosecutor becoming compromised, negligent, inefficient, incompetent or overworked, and the accused could well be discharged or charged with a lesser offence. It is therefore necessary to give the victims of crime a central role in the criminal justice system, failing which the victims will remain disillusioned and may even contemplate taking the law into their own hands. We have wondered so often whether we should have approached the courts at all to seek justice or if we should have just succumbed to the desire to take revenge for the sake of swift retribution.

Bail and no jail is the rule of law in our country. Every accused has the right to get bail, but the victims and their heirs do not have the right to oppose it, because that too is left entirely to the state. The accused is also given the benefit of the doubt when there is a faulty investigation by the prosecuting agency, because the rights of the accused take precedence over the victim's rights.

If there were no victims, would there be any need for the courts then? In our courts, there is a place for the accused, witnesses, defence counsels and the prosecution, but victims remain a neglected, eclipsed lot. In long-drawn legal battles, victims are often intimidated or humiliated, especially if the accused are rich and mighty. These tactics are adopted to discourage victims from attending court proceedings so the trial may follow the whims and fancies of the counsels of the accused. In the present system, the rights available to the victims are very limited and are grossly inadequate. Since it is the responsibility of the state to protect and safeguard the interests of the victims and witnesses, it is important to document the entire proceedings in the courtroom via audio and video recordings. This will deter the defence counsels from intimidating and humiliating the victims and the witnesses, and will ensure that the trial is conducted in a conducive atmosphere.

Some may argue that the recent amendment to the CrPC gives victims the right to appeal in higher courts. However, this is meaningless if the evidence is not led effectively during the trial, thus benefiting the accused.

Justice must not only be done—it must be seen to be done if it is to command public confidence. We believe that the more informed people are about the judicial system, the more confidence they will have in it. Protecting the interests of victims and witnesses must remain paramount.

Few people have personal or first-hand experience of court proceedings, or an overall understanding of the criminal justice system. Many people, therefore, base their views on how the system is portrayed on television or in films. These dramatized accounts seldom show what really happens in court. With the range of technology now available, it should be easier for people to access more information on court proceedings.

We believe that permitting people to see and hear court proceedings will increase their understanding of the judicial system without undermining the proper administration of justice. Most courts are open to the public and journalists report straight from court, unless the proceedings are in camera (a legal proceeding is considered 'in camera' when a hearing is held before the judge in private chambers or when the public is excluded from the courtroom). Despite this, very few people from the general public are actually able to witness court proceedings. For many, the criminal justice system is still seen as opaque, remote and difficult to understand.

In various countries, there are measures in place to televise court proceedings. An official copy of the recording should be given to all parties, including the victims. The recording of the proceedings should also be uploaded on the official website of the court. We also strongly feel that there should be a separate television channel on the lines of the Rajya Sabha and Lok Sabha channels for the courts, and the proceedings should be made accessible for public viewing.

These measures would enable the victims to follow up on cases when they are unable to be physically present for a hearing. Moreover, it will also familiarize the litigants with the functioning of the courts. After interacting with many litigants, we understood that they were not even aware of what had transpired in court. The counsels do not give them the true picture. In many cases, the counsels seek adjournments without the knowledge of their clients.

Another important factor which our administrators and prosecuting agencies must address is related to the quality of public prosecutors who represent the state. If the accused are wealthy and wield power, they always engage senior counsels and the public prosecutor is no match for them. It becomes the moral duty of the prosecuting agency to ensure that in such cases, they engage prosecutors of the same, if not greater, calibre. The conviction rate in our country is abysmally low thanks to poor representation from the state. We have been witness to many cases where the conduct of the public prosecutor sent shivers down our spine. In one of the cases in the Delhi High Court, we were shocked when we observed a standing counsel of the state, while arguing a murder case, was relying upon documents pertaining to another matter until the judge pointed out the same to him. Similarly, in another case, when the standing counsel was arguing his case, the investigating officer, who was present in court, pointed out that the facts he was referring to pertained to another case. Proper representation and presentation of the case is of prime importance in getting a quality judgment.

Due to the above reasons, we ensured that our case was represented well on behalf of the state and insisted that the CBI appoint a senior lawyer. We were fortunate as Harish N. Salve, the then solicitor general, agreed to represent the CBI. But he could not represent them for too long, for once Salve relinquished his post, he could not represent the CBI unless he was appointed by the Union of India. This was a major setback for us. Since the Ansals were being represented by some very senior counsels, we approached the CBI to re-appoint Salve. We were informed that since he was no longer the law officer, he could not represent the CBI unless he gave his consent to certain terms and conditions.

We were also told that the appointment had to be ratified by the Union of India.

Fortunately for us, Harish Salve, on the CBI's request, agreed and said that he and his junior, Aprajita Singh, would take up the case pro bono. Both of them were appointed to argue this case, as long as the matter was being heard in any court of law.

Our advice to all victims is that if they are up against a very powerful lobby, they must ensure that they are well represented by the state and also ensure they are present in court to keep track of the case and to assist the prosecuting agency. Another important factor is that the victims familiarize themselves with the documents and facts of the case. If the public prosecutor is missing some relevant facts, they should never hesitate to apprise him of the same. It is essential that the victims meet their counsels a day before the matter is listed, so the case can be refreshed. This practice plays a very significant role in the long run.

The nature of a criminal act leaves victims vulnerable and very often in need of assistance. Victims might find the legal process confusing and overwhelming. In India, victims have few legal rights and there are no victims' assistance programmes. On the other hand, there are special Acts in the European Union and the United States of America that protect the rights of victims.

The EU Act ensures that victims:
- are protected and treated with respect and dignity;
- are protected from further victimization and intimidation from the offender and further distress when they take part in the criminal justice process;
- receive appropriate support throughout proceedings and have access to justice;
- have appropriate access to compensation.

In the United States of America, under the Crime Victims' Rights Act 1984, a victim has the following rights:

- The right to be reasonably protected from the accused;
- The right to reasonable, accurate and timely notice of any public court proceeding, or any parole proceeding, involving the crime or of any release or escape of the accused;
- The right not to be excluded from any such public court proceeding, unless the court, after receiving clear and convincing evidence, determines that testimony by the victim would be materially altered if the victim heard other testimony at that proceeding;
- The right to be reasonably heard at any public proceeding in the district court involving release, plea, sentencing, or any parole proceeding;
- The reasonable right to confer with the attorney for the Government in the case;
- The right to full and timely restitution as provided in law;
- The right to proceedings free from unreasonable delay;
- The right to be treated with fairness and with respect for the victim's dignity and privacy.

The need of the hour is to protect the interests of victims and give them similar rights in our Indian justice system. This will not only restore people's faith, but also ensure equal participation of victims in the criminal justice system.

Afterword

For most people, home is a sanctuary that provides shelter, strength and comfort. For us, our home in south Delhi is both a sanctuary and a constant and agonizing reminder of the irreparable losses we have grappled with for the last nineteen years. Since 13 June 1997, my husband, Shekhar, and I have had to come to a home that has overpowering memories of our children, Unnati and Ujjwal, when we lost them on that black Friday.

It is a monument that houses their absence and the terrible finality of the horrific event that snatched them from us. Where once the laughter of our children welcomed us home from work, now a haunting silence surrounds us, never to be dispelled in this lifetime. It reminds us each day that the Uphaar fire was not a freak accident. It was a man-made disaster that was waiting to happen.

Had this tragedy not occurred, we would probably have been grandparents by now. Neither we nor the other victims of the fire would have had to go through the unimaginable trauma that we now suffer every single day.

Battered and bruised by our tragic loss, drifting between the urgent need to seek justice for the murder of our children, and dealing with the inevitable depression and melancholy that comes in the wake of such loss, we decided to write this book. We felt the need to share with readers the ordeal that an ordinary citizen must undergo should they decide to fight a legal battle. We would have liked to believe in the general perception that the judiciary, one of the four pillars of the Constitution, provides hope for the common man. Instead, we have experienced first-hand the bitter ground reality of how the system functions, its interminably long, laborious and unpredictable procedures. We have come to the terrible conclusion that justice is inaccessible for the common man. Justice is a luxury which only the rich and powerful and often, the corrupt, have access to. To quote Oliver Goldsmith, 'Law grinds the poor, rich men rule the law.'

Till 1997, our extremely limited understanding of the criminal justice system was naively based on its representations in film, where good always triumphs over evil. We had no way of knowing that, on the contrary, it is a Herculean task for victims to get justice in this country. The delivery system of the judiciary moves at a snail's pace and while our country has developed and evolved in several other spheres, the judiciary has not kept pace with its counterparts in other countries. As our struggle stretches on with very few signs of resolution in sight, we very seriously wondered whether it was worth going to court to seek justice if a victim has to wait for decades to receive it. By now we have cried ourselves hoarse repeating the phrase, 'Justice delayed is justice denied'. The cliché no longer seems to carry the sting it used to, because in our courts, the law is being administered for law's sake and not for the sake of justice.

We were novices who did not know the difference between a civil case and a criminal case. We had never entered the court premises before. When we took the decision to seek justice, we were discouraged by our lawyer friends and relatives, all of whom warned us that since the other party was extremely wealthy and had strong political connections, the case would most likely drag on for years. Yet, we plunged into a legal battle, full of hope even though our future without our children appeared desolate and lonely. We were even told that we would not be able to find a lawyer with the conviction required for a long-drawn legal battle. '*Kuch nahin hoga*' or 'nothing will happen' was the constant refrain we heard. Soon, we started referring to this attitude as the 'KNH' factor.

Despite the overarching pessimism, we did not lose hope and vowed that we would dedicate the remainder of our lives to getting justice for our children. We could not stop ourselves from being parents even though our children were no more, and we knew that as parents, it was our duty to get justice for our children. We realized that we had nothing to live for, but we did have a promise to keep even if it meant spending less time on our business. We started going to the court to follow up on the civil and criminal cases. We were repeatedly humiliated, insulted and threatened, but what the other side did not realize was that having lost our most precious possessions, we had nothing more to lose and hence, had become fearless. In fact, this attitude of the Ansals and their lawyers strengthened our resolve to take this legal battle to its conclusion. Sadly, the years have taught us that we committed a cardinal sin by just going to the court, hoping for justice.

But even as time dragged on, we never lost sight of our goal and remained focused. We have undergone unimaginable horror, a kind that is unthinkable for most people, and our trauma can never be assuaged.

Our bitter experiences have also taught us that our courts have an establishmentarian mindset, due to which economic offences are given priority over criminal cases, even those which involve death. The only time criminal cases are given priority is when there is public outrage or a media campaign surrounding a case. Though we constantly strove to stay strong for the sake of our children, we often experienced abject dejection when the courts gave out-of-turn hearings for cases that had attracted hype and media attention. It was almost as though our children were of a lesser god. Why else would politicians and the rich and influential get away with urgent hearings?

The Uphaar trial has stretched on for nineteen years and in these years, the country has witnessed many man-made disasters, where hundreds of lives have been lost. When we began this case, we had hoped that the courts would take up such cases on a priority basis to avoid similar tragedies in the future. But neither the government nor the judiciary took any cognizance of such cases. For the government, it was enough to announce a pitiful sum as ex gratia compensation and shy away from their actual responsibility of ensuring the safety and well-being of the common man.

Although courts exist to deliver justice for victims of crime, the truth is that the entire criminal trial is skewed in favour of the accused and the victims suffer the most. The irony being that if there were no victims, courts would not be required. And yet, no judge, though all of them must have been lawyers at some point in time and therefore well aware of the ground realities, has done anything to cultivate a culture in which the victims are treated with dignity or given a definite place in the criminal justice system. Despite being aware of this cruel reality, we gathered the courage to participate in court proceedings in a limited manner by approaching higher courts for an expeditious hearing, in spite of all the roadblocks that were created by the counsels for the defence.

In this ongoing battle for justice, the behaviour and the attitude of the defence lawyers representing the Ansals has been a cause of great pain and agony for us. While we hold no malice towards them for representing the Ansals, and we also understand their professional commitment towards their clients, we cannot forgive them for the personal attacks they made against us repeatedly. Perhaps, the realization that we were well versed with the facts of the case and were assisting the public prosecutor was such a cause of worry for them that they failed to remember that every counsel is an officer of the court and must maintain some degree of decorum. In the course of telling our story, we have not hesitated to reveal the ugliness and indignity we were personally subjected to by them.

On the other hand, our experience has also taught us that the entire legal fraternity cannot be painted with the same brush. We have also come across some deeply committed lawyers who have shown immense conviction in the case and have stood by our side in this epic battle for justice, one which has revealed the many chinks in several systems in our country. What makes the battle even more difficult for the victims is the poor quality of investigation. In the Uphaar case, despite the investigating agency having sufficient evidence to invoke section 304 (II) of the IPC, it chose to charge the Ansals with a lighter offence. During the trial, when the evidence was being laid out, it was very clear that it was a fit case for section 304 (II) IPC, but since the charge sheet had been filed under section 304 A IPC they could not be tried for a higher offence. It is our opinion that the investigating agency must file the charge sheet, citing a higher charge and leave it to the wisdom of the courts to decide upon it after the evidence has been examined.

We were under immense pressure from different quarters to withdraw the case and agree to an out-of-court settlement. But we are of the strong belief that any attempt to compromise would be another way of undermining the dignity of the dead.

Despite the numerous flaws in our criminal justice system, we have managed to overcome all the bottlenecks and obstacles. We had finally received a positive judgment from the Supreme Court, convicting the Ansals. Our stand had been vindicated and we now waited for the sentence to be awarded.

After waiting for seventeen months, the matter to decide the sentence for the Ansals came up before a three-judge bench of the Supreme Court on 19 August 2015. Shekhar and I stepped out of the Supreme Court of India that evening, consumed by a sense of outrage, loss and betrayal. The highest court in the land had just delivered the final verdict. We had hoped to return to our home with a sense of closure, if indeed, there can be any closure for a tragedy of such immeasurable proportions. Instead, what we heard was a judgment that, in one fell swoop, destroyed all our hopes of ever getting justice for our children. For nineteen interminably long years, we had struggled to keep going, doggedly pursuing a fiercely fought legal battle that stripped us of the time we could have had to ourselves, either to grieve or to try and pick up the scattered fragments of our lives.

Pursuing the legal options open to us, we had single-mindedly focused our energies on seeking justice for the fifty-nine innocent victims of the Uphaar tragedy. In these nineteen years, we had never permitted ourselves the luxury of shedding a single tear in public, even under the most trying circumstances. But on 19 August 2015, as we stood outside the court after hearing the verdict, tears streamed down my face as if they would never stop. We had been let down by the very system on which we had pinned all our hopes. The Ansal brothers were set to walk free instead of being incarcerated for their crime, on the grounds that they were too old for a prison sentence. In lieu of their freedom, they would pay a penalty of Rs 60 crore to the Delhi government, which would be utilized to build a trauma centre.

Unable to sleep even a wink that night, our thoughts moved manically from extreme despair to intense anger. Nothing could provide us solace or comfort, as our minds raced back and forth, through these long and arduous years where we went to court every single day, just to seek justice for Ujjwal and Unnati. Once again, we survived, even though we did not want to, because we realized through the haze of our pain that the battle against the wealthy, powerful and corrupt must go on. Through the agony of those hours and days following the judgment, we faced the camera and the media for reactions and responses. Yet again, we answered phone calls from the media, from concerned citizens following the case, and from a handful of friends, and prepared for battle again and for the telling of this tragic story. Indeed, this is not the story of a single personal tragedy. It is not only the story of the loss of our lovely children. It is an epic story of many tragedies, of betrayals and let-downs, because it exposes the shocking truths and insensitivities that riddle our society, our judicial system and our policymakers. It is, therefore, a story that must be told and we have attempted to do so to the best of our abilities.

Acknowledgements

As in every hour of our lives, we thank our beloved children, Unnati and Ujjwal, whose memories inspire us to continue fighting for justice against all odds. We would never have been able to write this book, filled as it is with some unbearably painful memories, had we not known in our hearts that they would have wanted us to share our story with readers.

Our dear friends Shubha Mudgal and Aneesh Pradhan not only inspired us, but also helped in the creation of this book. In particular, we are deeply indebted to Shubha for having read the first draft of the manuscript and for sharing her candid comments with us. Our close friendship has been reflected in the support and encouragement she has provided us through these long and arduous years.

We thank Dr Ravi Berry and Nera Berry for supporting our decision to pen our journey for justice, and for offering us invaluable advice and suggestions.

My sister, Manjula Saxena, stood by us through the difficult years, starting 1997. Without her, we would have all but lost the unconditional support that is usually provided only by family.

The seemingly unending legal battle fought by the Association of Victims of Uphaar Fire Tragedy (AVUT) would probably have ended even before it began had it not been for the contribution of senior advocate K.T.S. Tulsi, who led us in this crusade. The knowledge and wisdom he imparted have been of great help and support through these interminably long years. We are unable to find words to adequately express our gratitude to him and his dedicated team of lawyers, including Hari Pillai. We would also like to express our deep gratitude to senior advocates K. Sultan Singh and Vikas Pahwa for their invaluable contributions. We also remain indebted to our advocates on record, Rishi Malhotra and Jayant Mehta. All of the above-mentioned legal experts extended unparalleled generosity by representing AVUT pro bono, for which we thank them from the core of our hearts.

We are very obliged to senior advocates Harish N. Salve and Aprajita Singh for their commitment towards the case. They had taken up the case pro bono for the Central Bureau of Investigation (CBI).

We also thank the members of AVUT for reposing their faith in us.

There are several individuals who were moved so intensely by the tragedy and by our unending search for justice, that they went out of their way to help us both formally and informally. Naming each of them will not be possible, but we are immensely grateful for their help and support.

We thank the court reporters, both in print and electronic media, who were relentless and extremely dedicated while reporting the court proceedings in the case.

This book would not have been possible had it not been for Kanishka Gupta from Writer's Side for representing us as our literary agent and for helping us find a suitable publisher. We are also thankful to Achala Upendran, who edited our book on behalf of Writer's Side.

Penguin Random House India very kindly agreed to publish this book and instilled confidence in us, which we needed as first-time authors. We are grateful to Vaishali Mathur, who patiently waited for us to submit the final manuscript and edited the book further. We would like to acknowledge with gratitude the contribution of Jyotsna Raman from the Penguin Random House team, who scoured the manuscript with an eagle eye during the editing process.

To the many individuals who have supported us, we offer sincere thanks. And to the many others who made our journey difficult and challenging, we offer more thanks. Had it not been for them, the frailties of the judicial and criminal justice systems would not have been so starkly evident to us. They helped expose the rot and injustices inherent in our systems, compelling us to take on the corruption head-on and without fear.